Making Money
In
Dominican Real Estate

Your Complete Guide to Investing in the DR

By Anthony Almeida

Walden Books

First Published in Paperback 2008
By Walden Books

A catalogue record is for this book is available from the US Library

Design and Typeset by Jeffrey Posner

Printed and bound by Lulu

Cover picture used with permission from the author.

ISBN: 978-0-6152-3859-3

Walden Books
NY8, NY

ACKNOWLEDGEMENTS

I'd like to acknowledge my previous partners at Caribbean Reality Investment group, Daryl Bryant, William Halick, and Matt Mayernick for giving me the idea and initial encouragement to undertake this project.

I'd like to thank my girlfriend Martha for pushing me through the periods where I had completely become exhausted by the topic at hand and almost given up. Without her support (nagging) this book may very well still be a file on my computer.

I'd like to thank my father whose interest in international real estate ignited the passion I've grown to have towards it.

I'd like to thank my mother, who believed in my abilities and pushed me to pursue my dreams…

To Chris Almeida, Jeffrey Posner, Chris Azzari, Justin Buffer, who all in some way or another helped me on a day to day basis allowing me to go off and do what I do best.

Table of Contents

Chapter 1

Why Invest in the Dominican Republic

The fact that you've bought a book on Dominican Republic real estate shows me that you already have a degree of interest in purchasing property on the magical island. Maybe you've read the news reports about the up and coming property market on the still affordable Caribbean island or maybe you've visited the island and decided it was a place you could see yourself retiring to.

Whatever your interest in Dominican Republic real estate stems from, it is my goal in this chapter to present to you a great case for following that interest from an initial idea to ownership of property in the Dominican Republic, or as the natives fondly calls it, The DR.

In this chapter I will show you why The Dominican Republic makes sense as a place to own property for both; those looking for an investment vehicle, and those looking for a vacation or retirement home. I will present a case as to why vacation homes are fast becoming favorable investments for baby boomers, and why the Dominican Republic will fast become the most sought after vacation home destination of this very group.

Where will the baby boomers put their money?

This is a reasonable question to ask yourself as you ponder the credentials for your investment criteria. The largest generation of money spending consumers is nearing retirement.

Approximately 35% of all home sales in 2004 were second-home purchases, and baby boomers make up the majority of buyers for this growing trend. Boomers have both the means and the motivation to take advantage of the attractive housing market, and they represent a high percentage of the population.

Boomers, who were born between 1946 and 1964, now aged 44 to 62, definitely have the means. They are in their peak earning years and many are also equity-rich, with homes that have appreciated significantly over time. Match that buying power with low interest rates, and they are in a prime position to buy a second and sometimes even a third home. Many of them remember 18% interest rates of the early '80s, making today's environment even more attractive.

Baby boomers also have the motivation, buying for vacation, investment, and other reasons. They may be planning to retire in a few years and want to lock in rapidly escalating prices now at low interest rates to buy a home that serves as a short-term vacation residence and a future retirement home. Or they intend to work for several more years, but are seeking an appealing recreational attraction in the meantime for their children and grandchildren to enjoy holiday weekends and vacations.

In many cases, boomers are opting for vacation properties they can enjoy in the off-season and rent out during peak vacation months, with the goal of covering expenses while the property appreciates. They may share such purchases with other family members to accomplish their objectives. Builders have created or partnered with property management companies to handle rentals and absentee ownership details for such buyers.

How will the housing slump affect real estate investment?

In a recent Wall Street Journal article, June Fletcher reports "The housing slump has sent many Americans shopping south of the border.

Existing-home prices in the U.S. dropped 4.5% in the third quarter from a year ago, according to S&P/Case-Shiller. But they are still climbing in much of Latin America and the Caribbean.

Buyers are being enticed by the kind of double-digit appreciation that has all but disappeared in the States. In addition, a growing number of new developments are targeting Americans looking for good deals and a lower cost of living.

Since 2003, annual home-price appreciation has been running at 20% in the Dominican Republic, and could reach 50% in the near future, according to Boomerang Unlimited, a Napa, Calif., real-estate investment advisory firm."

As you can see real estate will always be favored form of investment for its well known advantages over other vehicles. Americans will continue to pour their money into real estate. The only difference is that they now have more options of where to purchase.

Fletcher writes "Still, the rapid appreciation is drawing growing numbers of bargain hunters, making good deals scarcer and causing some customers to look beyond the usual vacation hot spots. In the Dominican Republic, Century 21 broker Dean Brown says that 80% of his buyers this year have been Americans, compared with half last year."

Europeans have always seen the potential to turn huge profits in Dominican Republic real estate. Americans are now opening their eyes to see the same potential. And as America wakes up to this the growth and numbers will multiply way beyond what was seen from the Europeans.

U.S. Dominican Relations

The U.S. has a strong interest in a democratic, stable, and economically healthy Dominican Republic. The country's standing as the largest Caribbean economy, second-largest country in terms of population and land mass, with large bilateral trade with the United States, and its proximity to the United States and other smaller Caribbean nations make the Dominican Republic an important partner in hemispheric affairs. The Embassy estimates that 100,000 U.S. citizens live in the Dominican Republic; many are dual nationals. An important element of the relationship between the two countries is the fact that more than 1 million individuals of Dominican origin reside in the United States, most of them in the metropolitan Northeast and some in Florida.

U.S. relations with the Dominican Republic are excellent, and the U.S. has been an outspoken supporter of that country's democratic and economic development. The Dominican Government has been supportive of many U.S. initiatives in the United Nations and related agencies. The two governments cooperate in the fight against the traffic in illegal substances. The Dominican Republic has worked closely with U.S. law enforcement officials on issues such as the extradition of fugitives and measures to hinder illegal migration.

The United States supports the Fernández administration's efforts to improve Dominican competitiveness, to attract foreign private investment, to fight corruption, and to modernize the tax system. Bilateral trade is important to both countries. U.S. firms, mostly manufacturers of apparel, footwear, and light electronics, as well as U.S. energy companies, account for much of the foreign private investment in the Dominican Republic.

Proximity to the United States

Even with the extremely positive relations the United States shares with the Dominican Republic the fact remains that the United States is still in its infancy in regards to its use of the Dominican Republic as a vacation getaway.

Though there has always been a stalwart set of real-estate buyers and vacationers who have been happy with the DR, the bulk of its tourist trade is not the typical North American set traditionally dominating most Caribbean islands. Of the 4 million tourists visiting the country each year, only about half come from the United States. Another 600,000 are Dominican expatriates coming home to visit relatives. The remaining 2 million tourists are from Europe, frequenting the many all-inclusive resorts located throughout the country. Many Americans don't realize that there are more hotel rooms for rent in the D.R. than in any other Caribbean country. The U.S. tourist numbers, however, are poised to change.

The Dominican Republic is just too easy to get to from the United States for it to be ignored. A plane ride from JFK airport in New York will have you in the Dominican Republic in less than 3 hours. That flight is only a tiny bit longer than Miami. And the country is extremely accessible once landing on the island. If your plane landed in Puerto Plata airport you could be at your condo in fifteen minutes. Many Caribbean islands don't give you that luxury.

Several major airlines offer regular service into several cities in the DR, from cities in both North America and Europe. From the U.S. and Canada, Continental, American Airlines, and TWA have direct flights to the DR. Regular flights are available from Europe via Air France, Air Europe, American Airlines, Lufthansa and Iberia. The DR has 7 international airports, the three largest of which are in Puerto Plata, Santo Domingo and Punta Cana.

Has the Dominican Republic responded to the increasing interest in their real estate?

Robert Snijder thinks so. He says, "The Dominican government recognizes that Foreign Investment contributes to the economic growth and social development of the country insofar as they favor the generation of jobs and foreign currency, promote the process of capitalization and provide efficient production, marketing and management methods.

"This can be seen by the policy regarding foreign currency and taxes, where legislation provides an attractive legal framework for foreign investors. Law 158 on Foreign Investment allows unlimited foreign investment in nearly all sectors of the economy. In October 2001 this was extended to make investment in business and upscale tourism exempt from income tax for 10 years. As a new development all investors will benefit from 10 years of tax free status "no taxes payable on capital gain rental revenue".

Next to this any type of foreign investors shall have the right to buy through commercial banks the foreign currency needed to remit abroad, in freely-convertible currencies, the total amount of invested capital and the dividends declared during each fiscal period, up to the total amount of the net current profits of the period, upon payment of income tax, including the capital gains made and registered in the books of the company according to generally accepted accounting practices.

The property taxes are very moderate like: Properties held in the name of an individual are subject to an annual property tax ("IPI") of 1% of government-appraised value in excess of RD$5,000,000 pesos (± USD150,000) except for lots without construction or farms outside city limits. If the property is held by a

10

corporation, no property tax is due. Instead, the corporation must pay a 1% tax on corporate assets. However, any income tax paid by the corporation will constitute a credit toward the tax on assets, so that if corporate income taxes paid are equal to or higher than the taxes on assets due, the corporation will have no obligation to pay taxes on its assets."

The Dominica Republic is clearly encouraging foreign investment in their local real estate. They are not only making it easy for foreigners to invest in real estate, they are making it profitable.

DanDannyDaniel of Dominican Paradise speaks extremely highly of his experience with the Dominican Republic government's response to the ever increasing presence of foreign investment in their country. "I've studied emerging markets for over a year. I read everything I could read, I attended seminars in many cities, and I even went for five days to the National Association of Realtors convention in New Orleans. This was held in November '06.

While at this convention, I spent my entire time in the International Pavilion. I looked at Real Estate opportunities in every nook and cranny of our globe. I took this stuff back to my room at night and poured over the literature and I kept narrowing my choices down…and kept narrowing and kept narrowing…until…

I landed here, in the Dominican Republic…and not only here, but on the Samana Peninsula on the famed North Coast. I believe this to be one of the top 2 or 3 Real Estate opportunities in the world today and that its close (< 2 hour plane ride from Miami) proximity to the US definitely puts it at number one for anyone in the Western Hemisphere.

I've been living here off and on for over a year now (first trip February, '07) and permanently since mid July, 2007 and you know what I've discovered?? I've discovered that almost everything I studied, read and heard has come true.

I was told we would have a new International Airport…well; we have one at El Catey. American Airlines is already doing daily flights there from Miami (via Puerto Rico) and I just heard this week Jet Blue has direct flights from New York!

I was told we would have a new road connecting this new airport to Las Terrenas and the Samana Peninsula and it has already been cleared.

I was told we would have a new road connecting the capital of Santo Domingo in the south to the Samana Peninsula and though it is not paved entirely people are already driving it. This cuts what was about a 4 hour drive down to about 1 ½ hours!

I was told we would have new golf courses and several are already being built and several more have been approved.

I was told we would have a marina and land has already been purchased, cleared and even rivers moved. Talk about your Dubai-like scale!

I was told we would see an increase in Cruise travel and that is happening. We went from 2-4 cruise ships a week in season to now over 10 a week.

I was told we would have new water treatment facility and pipeline and that's 75% done.

I was told we would have new sewer treatment and city sewer and that's nearly complete.

Other things like Fee Simple Land title (you actually OWN your purchase), awesome tax benefits, new medical and dental facilities, American Engineering firms, Architects and designers all flocking here. Environmental obligations are being embraced. Education is at the top of every politicians mind."

Where in the Dominican Republic is a good place to buy property?

It is my intention throughout this book to empower you with the knowledge to make an informed decision of where in the Dominican Republic it makes most sense for you to purchase property.

In Chapter 2 "Understanding the layout of the island" I will take you on a written tour of the entire island. I'll discuss which beaches are contained in the different geographical areas of the island, and what you can expect in terms of scenery, culture, living, and activity in each particular region. The overview of the regions will give you a place to begin. The areas that spark the greatest amount of your attention will be a solid place to start. The island is large and diverse and there is really "that special place" for every type of personality.

Along with knowledge of the Island itself, you will also need to decide which type of property you intend to purchase. Different areas of the island are better suited for particular interests. In chapter 4 "Evaluating the different types of real estate" I will present the different forms real estate investment available in the Dominican Republic. I'll discuss the differences and present the advantages and disadvantages of each.

Chapters 5-7 will discuss how money is made in real estate investments, how economic cycles affect real estate investment, and how to find and evaluate properties for investment. The better understanding you have about how the Dominican Real Estate market works, the easier it will be for you to determine your ultimate plan of action.

The rest of the book will focus on the details of a real estate transaction in the Dominican Republic, owning property, gaining profit from your investment, up keeping your investment, and will answer just about any question you may have in regards to your plan of owning real estate in the Caribbean.

Which areas are currently hot?

While it is ultimately up to you to decide where to buy in the Dominican Republic I don't think it would be fair not to leave you with some concrete examples of areas that booming as interest in the country goes.

The areas that I mention below are by no means the only regions seeing strong growth. And there is no guarantee that these particular areas will lead the country through the next decade. But I think it is important for you see the factors that have led to the increasing interest in these areas. Even if you decide not to purchase in these areas you will have the knowledge of what investors look for, and apply that knowledge and criteria to any area you're interested in.

When you talk to real estate professionals throughout the Dominica Republic certain areas are repeatedly suggested as "the place to buy." While you always have to take into context who you are speaking to, it's hard to ignore the praise that areas such Las Terrenas on the Samana Peninsula, and the area fondly nicknamed "the Amber Coast" in the north.

These areas, which all possess their own unique beauty and investment potential, all share the distinction of beginning to attract the eyes of investors all over the world.

Las Terrenas

I asked Bruce Pierson of Dominican Paradise.com why he felt that Las Terrenas was beginning to hear the whispers of interest from investors throughout the world and how long he felt before the world awakened to opportunities that are present there.

Bruce writes "Unlike many of the coastal towns in the Dominican Republic, Las Terrenas has been mostly undiscovered by major economic tourism and development. The Peninsula of Samaná was mainly an eco-tourism destination and the perfect hideaway for many Europeans expats.

Most of the desired real estate is not owned yet by foreign investors or all-inclusive hotel chains; instead much of it is still owned by Dominican families and is still affordable.

This is about to change. The new international airport, El Catey (25 minutes drive from Las Terrenas), is now operational. Long distance carriers from Europe and The Americas are now bringing tourists directly in the Samaná Peninsula.

In May 2005 construction began on the new Santo Domingo - Samaná Highway that will reduce the drive time from 5 hours to less than 90 minutes.

In the past year alone, 4 all-inclusive, 5 star Bahia Principe resorts have opened in the peninsula, with a total of 1,600 rooms. The major project "Las Terrenas Country Club" is already under construction and selling its villas and condos on the golf course, designed by the world renowned Dye family.

A marina project, called Puerto Bonito, with 150 slips, is also under construction near Las Terrenas

Chains such as Wyndham and Meliá have acquired properties and options on several of the available land plots, narrowing the window of available real estate in the area.

We believe that there is a 3 to 6 year window of opportunity to purchase land for development in the area of Las Terrenas, and, the sooner the better. It is likely that 2 to 3 years after completion of the new international airport and highway, the prices of real estate will have drastically increased, catching up to and equaling the other Caribbean Islands.

In addition to the developments and chains mentioned above, more than 20 more projects are currently underway in Samaná. Presently, investing in Las Terrenas is not only about investing in one of the most beautiful areas in the Caribbean, but also about the possibility of getting an excellent ROI. We foresee land prices will continue rising, minimum, at a yearly rate of about 35%. Compared to the low rates of ROI in Europe and the US, this signifies great potential for earnings with minimal risk."

I spoke a great deal with Bruce, who moved Las Terrenas twenty years ago. His interest and love for the area goes far beyond financial and economical interest. "The DR is arguably the most beautiful spot in the Caribbean, referred to by many as "The Land of Dreams". Las Terrenas boasts a magical strip of 15 kilometers of virgin beach, and a town with more than 40 international restaurants including everything from Italian, French, and Swiss cuisine to Japanese sushi bars. It offers as well a broad selection of available activities including horseback riding, golf, scuba diving, windsurfing, tennis and many more within just minutes of town."

Bruce, who has made the Las Terrenas his own, sees the area as an unspoiled paradise where the inhabitants ride motorcycles instead of cars, and all share a sense of community that makes it a magical place to raise a family. Bruce, who spent time with the Peace Corps and has traveled a majority of the world is not hesitant to pronounce Las Terrenas "One of the most magical places I've been to."

And as others come to see the same unique qualities that Bruce has, you can't help but to realize that there is a premium to be paid for paradises like this.

The Amber Coast

Featuring the popular towns of Puerto Plata, Cabarete and Sosua, the north coast has been referred to as the Amber Coast due to the prevalence of this semi-precious gem. This area is quite different than the more secluded and sleepy hideaway of Las Terrenas. Puerto Plata, Cabarete and Sosua already possess all inclusive super resorts like Breezes. They have an influx of college-aged travelers heading down to Caberete for its world famous kite surfing, and the single traveler heading to Sosua for its equally famous potential for romance.

Between Sosúa and Cabarete you will find many lovely expanses of beaches, including Perla Marina, Seahorse Ranch, Encuentro, Punta Goleta, Kite Beach, Playa Laguna, and others. This area is home to many of the area's residential districts, both along the beach and high in the hills with an ocean or mountain view. Many foreigners have invested here

Nikki Simon, of Coral Bay Real Estate, feels strongly about the Dominican Republic's potential for investment profit, the north coast in particular:

"The Dominican Republic (DR) in general and the North Coast in particular present an excellent investment climate for foreign owners. Real estate values in the DR are perhaps the best in the Caribbean as affordable prices, low taxes, and direct commercial and charter flights provide varied and affordable access from multiple US, Canadian, and European cities into Puerto Plata or Santiago airports. Once here, beachfront and close proximity apartments range from approximately 100K US to over a million dollars dependent upon size, luxury and location but very nice affordable values can be easily identified through mainstream realtors such as RE/MAX Coral Bay. Houses tend to be more in gated communities but offer stunning views from mountain and beachfront vistas.

Values on the Amber Coast are further enhanced by its location on the north side of the island which offers amazing diving and wind sports such as kite surfing and boarding, even holding world championships in Cabarete each June.

The DR government and the IMF are investing heavily in the infrastructure of the country in preparation for years of further growth and attraction of retiring Baby Boomers. Electricity, road, sewage, and police investments all are improving conditions at a regular pace and new tax laws promote first time retirement real estate investment and residency by awarding significant tax savings. The DR-CAFTA treaty with the US now will promote even greater trade with the US for this stable democracy bringing in more goods and services while positioning the DR as a manufacturing and trade hub with China and Latin American countries looking to take advantage of the DR's tariff advantages with the US as they ship materials and assembled goods through the DR."

Daryl Bryant of Mydrlife.com says "You're going to see the North Coast continue to become a prominent destination for foreigners to purchase real estate over the next five years. What you're seeing now is a shortage of available villas which is causing the values of villas to rise drastically, especially ocean front. In a few years you'll be seeing the same thing happen to the value of condos."

I asked Daryl Bryant what makes The North Coast so attractive to investors.

He responded, "It has everything the baby boomers want. It's only an hour longer of a flight than Florida; it has gorgeous beaches, restaurants, bars, big hotels, and small hotels… everything Aruba has at a third of the price. People are realizing this. In ten years people are going to be talking about 'the day's real estate was still affordable on The Amber Coast."

Chapter 2

Understanding the layout of the island

There is a famous clichéd saying in real estate that the three most important things to consider when making a real estate investment is "location, location, location." There is a reason that you've probably heard this saying before. The reason is; because it's true!

When I first decided to invest in international real estate I made the same mistake that most people do. I was interested in purchasing in Brazil at the time. I had been to a few of the major hot spots and every time I decided that I was ready to settle on a destination for investment, I would talk to a local who would tell me of an even better, more charming, more prestigious, part of the country.

This leads me to my first word of advice: "No matter where you decide to invest there will always be other places that may be better." It is a fact of life that the grass is always greener. There will always be a new up and coming area. Do not make the mistake of waiting for the perfect place and time to buy. It will never come and years from now you will be saying, "Man if I had only bought...."

The trick is to due thorough adequate research. After doing the research, you narrow down your choices. You weigh your options. Then when you have decided on a location you do more research about that particular location until you find the specific street or section of town you want to buy in.

Since most of you reading this book are interested in purchasing in the Dominican Republic and most likely do not live there, you will have to do a majority of your research from your computer or over a telephone. You will also have to learn to trust those you employ to help you on your quest to purchase in the DR. You will also have to learn to trust your instincts. Something is telling you to buy real estate on the island. Trust that intuition. Through your course of researching the Dominican Republic you may come across information on Panama, or Costa Rico, or Brazil, or Jamaica... and while all of these may also be great places to invest, remember that you have narrowed down your location to the Dominican. At this point, second guessing yourself will only hinder and interfere with your time researching.

Beginning your research

Now that you've decided on the Dominican Republic as the Caribbean island that you would like to own property on, you must begin to learn a little bit more about your options.

The Dominican Republic is part of the largest island in the Caribbean. In the section that follows I am going to break the island down into different regions. Choosing a specific region is the first step in your research.

In an ideal world you would have the time and money to travel to each of these regions and do your own personal explorations. Unfortunately this is seldom possible for most people. I also do not recommend it because it can become overwhelming.

What is a more practical plan is to learn a little bit about each region of the island and decide which region suits your needs the best.

I will try to be as unbiased as possible in my including descriptions of each of the regions. As the entire Dominican has its own beauty and charm. An entire book can be written about each region, but my intention with these descriptions is just to wet your appetite and give you a possible direction in which you can focus your attention and research.

The regions

Diverse terrain and extraordinary natural beauty is a hallmark of the Dominican Republic's six regions. The fantastic combination of environments will capture your imagination and refresh your soul.

Rolling mountains, lush jungles, pine forest, coral reefs, unspoiled beaches, and arid desert co-exist side-by-side in this magical land. The magnificence of nature sets the scene for quaint villages, charming cities, and first class accommodations for visitors.

The Central Region

Home to some of the country's lushest and most fertile lands, the central region of the Dominican Republic includes the towns of Santiago and La Vega, as well as the stunning Cordillera Central mountain ranges and the Cibao Valley. Well endowed with rich soil and incredible natural resources, this region regularly attracts nature lovers, cigar connoisseurs and adventurers.

La Vega

A quiet town with a rich history, La Vega was also blessed with fertile soil and precious gold. It is fairly quaint, with 60,000 inhabitants. However, when February rolls around, the city is anything but quiet and reserved. La Vega is the home of Carnaval, one of the oldest and most vibrant of Dominican traditions.

With the colorful yet devilish masks worn and created by attendees, the Dominicans get rowdy and celebrate the victory of good over evil. A matchless celebration, both natives and non-residents freely dance through the streets to blaring, energetic music while sampling the finest food and drink the Dominican Republic has to offer.

Santiago

Often compared to Santo Domingo, the city of Santiago, the second largest metropolis, is comprised of natives that prefer a less chaotic and more purposeful lifestyle than its counterpart. Home to over 750,000 people, the heart of this laid back city proves to be the cultured downtown area. In addition, Santiago is where most of the country's presidents were raised; giving the city well-deserved bragging rights.

A primary downtown attraction and a place were boredom is not in the vocabulary is Calle del Sol. Known as the city's main shopping district, the street is stocked with shops, hotels, restaurants, bars and an array of vendors.

Located north of Calle del Sol is Parque Duarte. A popular area to kick up those traveling feet and get acquainted with the natives, this shady park is a great representation of Santiago's laid back lifestyle.

An ideal spot for cigar lovers and a perfect place to relax after a day of shopping is the Museo del Tabaco. Visitors will learn about the art of cigar-making while purchasing some of the country's top brands. Located in Santiago, it would be a sin to exit Cibao Valley without stopping by this one-of-a-kind museum.

People from around the globe visit Santiago year-round to stay at some of the finest accommodations that satisfy the needs of any traveler. In addition, the city provides a vibrant nightlife and variety of stores that are comparable to the capital city.

Most travelers know that convenience is an added bonus. Santiago provides an additional benefit by serving as an alternate airport to Puerto Plata. Also, both of the airports are of about equal distance to Monte Cristi and other destinations in the Dominican Republic's northwest region.

The East Coast

The East Coast region contains the most popular and fastest growing tourist area in the country – Punta Cana/Bavaro. One look at the surroundings and there is no question as to why. This is the place to be if tourists are seeking an all-inclusive style vacation set on one of the most picturesque beaches in the world.

Vacationers don't have to travel far for a change of scenery. Just south of the thriving area is environmentally forward Bayahibe. This area not only contains one of the most celebrated national parks, but has also received two awards for its conservation efforts in tourism.

Another popular east coast destination is La Romana. Most people who know a thing or two about the Dominican Republic instantly think of Casa de Campo when asked about this quaint area. While the luxurious resort frequented by many celebrities is a top attraction, the city of La Romana is historically important, especially for baseball fans, and worth a visit.

Punta Cana and Bavaro

In Punta Cana, it's all about the beach. Punta Cana is undeniably breathtaking with tall swaying palms scattered along 21 miles of some of the whitest and finest coral sand beaches in the world. The area has become a haven for vacationers who are seeking a beach chair, a Pina Colada and a good read.

Punta Cana is the perfect atmosphere for families, couples, or friends who are looking for a resort-style vacation. Just about every tour embarks from this area so no one in the group can complain about being bored.

The majority of the over 30 resorts in Punta Cana are all-inclusive, allowing for an easygoing vacation with plenty to do. As one of the fastest growing areas in the country, more luxurious and bigger complexes are planned to open in 2006. Beyond new accommodations, a 24-mile long boulevard is being built to easily move vacationers throughout the area.

La Romana

Known for its sugar factories, the area of La Romana is one of the more industrialized in the Dominican Republic. In fact, it's the sugar that makes La Romana and neighboring San Pedro de Macoris two of the leading Major League Baseball player producing towns.

During the six months when sugar is not in high production, workers often compete in baseball games against other sugar mill workers. This has helped to brew the excitement and passion for baseball that has become synonymous with the country. Baseball fans will want to take in a game at the Michelin Baseball Stadium located at the city's west end. The home team is the La Romana Azucareros, which translates to La Romana Sugar Bowls. Tickets range from $50-$150.

To the northeast of the stadium is the Mercado Municipal, an open-air marketplace spanning several city blocks where tourists can purchase fresh produce and shop for crafts and souvenirs.

Casa de Campo

Casa de Campo is considered one of the most complete and luxurious resort communities in the Caribbean. Many celebrities vacation at the complex such as George Hamilton, Bill Clinton, Shakira, Elizabeth Taylor, former President George H. Bush, and the country's very own Sammy Sosa.

PGA golf greats including Dana Quigley, Jim Thorpe, Ed Dougherty and Tom Wargo have all made their way to Casa de Campo to play Teeth of the Dog, the first course to open at the resort nearly 30 years ago. Since creating Teeth of the Dog, Pete Dye has designed Links and his newest course Dye Fore. While this new course is receiving rave reviews from international golfers, Teeth of the Dog is still a favorite and for this reason the resort has invested in its extensive makeover.

In addition to golf, the resort also has a full-service marina capable of accommodating yachts up to 250-feet long with its new expansion. The full-service marina is encapsulated by international boutiques, jewelers, galleries and flavorful restaurants.

The resort has a variety of accommodations from spacious guestrooms with balconies overlooking the golf course to luxury suites brushed with Caribbean flair. Lavish villas ranging from two to six bedrooms provide an elite option for families and groups of friends. Villas come complete with private pool, personal touring car and dedicated maid and butler who will prepare and serve breakfast daily among catering to other requests.

Beyond golf, yachts and living the life of luxury, Casa de Campo also features a polo club, private beach, pool and spa area, horseback riding, sport shooting, tennis and meeting facilities.

Altos de Chavon

Built in 1976, Altos de Chavon is a cobblestone lined replica of a quaint 16th century Tuscan hillside village. Set high above the Chavon River, this cultural center features shops, restaurants, artist's studios and galleries housed in stone and coral block buildings. The complex also features a school of design, an open-air amphitheater, an archeology museum, and art gallery.

The semi-circled 5,000 seat amphitheater practically turns back time thanks to its Grecian qualities. This limestone concert bowl was inaugurated by Frank Sinatra and Carlos Santana in 1982 and has since hosted dozens of concerts, symphonies, theatrical events and festivals. International recording artists Julio Iglesias, Dizzy Gillespie, Air Supply and Gloria Estefan have played under the stars to adoring fans at this one-of-a-kind amphitheater.

The country's most famous fashion designer, Oscar de La Renta, is intimately involved in the Altos de Chavon School of Design. In addition to fashion design, the two-year Associate in Applied Science degree program has concentrations in graphic design, interior design and fine arts/illustration. The controlled curriculum was developed in conjunction with the world renowned Parsons School of Design, which accepts graduates to complete their four-year degree.

The Center also has an artist-in-residence program in which established and up-and-coming artists live and work in Altos de Chavon for three months. Painters, sculptors, photographers, writers, musicians and architects exchange knowledge in open studios throughout the village. Past artists have included author Julia Alvarez and artists Henry Koerner and Roberto Juarez.

Bayahibe

A small fishing village, Bayahibe is gaining recognition as a growing tourism destination and as an environmental benchmark for the Dominican Republic and the Caribbean.

There are several all-inclusive hotels in Bayahibe including Viva Resort by Wyndham and Coral by Hilton. The village is comprised of restaurants serving fresh seafood, dive shops, pastel-colored huts, and a few smaller hotels.

Visitors can truly mingle with the locals as several rent out their homes as guest houses for under $25 a night. This is especially attractive to backpackers who use the village as a base camp for exploring Parque Nacional del Este, a 172-square mile national park known for its 200 caves dating from pre-Columbian time.

The hotels of Bayahibe have made a conscious decision to preserve their environment as it welcomes more tourists. They've banded together to create an area worthy of the Green Globe Award, part of an international program which recognizes organizations that make a significant contribution to sustainable development.

The award is monitored by the Caribbean Action for Sustainable Tourism (CAST) and supported by the Caribbean Hotel Association (CHA). Hoteliers receive the Green Globe when they have met international standards for waste prevention, reuse and recycling practices and preservation of the surroundings.

Current environmental projects include: protecting the ocean floor, creating educational programs for hotel personnel and residents of Bayahibe, protection of endangered turtles and iguanas, and fostering children's awareness through the group of Bayahibe Wardens.

The area holds a second environmental preservation award which stands proudly on the beach, the Blue Flag. Governed by the Foundation for Environmental Education (FEE), the DR is one of 33 countries whose beaches have been recognized for maintaining high water quality, developing environmental education programs, environmental management, safety and other ecologically sound services.

For visitors looking for a little metropolitan flare, day trips to Santo Domingo and the Mediterranean village of Altos de Chavon can be arranged through the hotel or one of the several tour operators.

Since owning real estate near or on the beach is a huge reason why people decide to purchase in the Dominican Republic I will list all the beaches contained in each region. One way to narrow down to search is to eventually decide which beach you want to be near within a particular region.

Here are the beaches in the East Coast region:

Isla Catalina
Only six square miles in size and located just off the shore from Bayahibe, Isla Catalina features the best coral reef in the area, a mangrove swamp and sand dunes. Crowds of tourists come for a day of scuba diving and relaxation.

Isla Saona
Located within Parque Nacional Del Este, Isla Saona is one of the southeast coast's most popular tourist destinations. In fact, this small island was recently named one of the Caribbean's Eight Dream Beaches by *Caribbean Travel & Life magazine*. Powder sugar beaches, towering palms, azure water and the occasional sand bar at low tide make this one of the DR's most romantic destinations.

Playa Bavaro
Just north of Punta Cana, the Bavaro resort area continues the long stretch of picture perfect white beach. While Playa Bavaro is considered a separate beach from Punta Cana, the area appears as one extend strip of fluffy white sand reaching over 30 miles along the coast. Like Punta Cana, Bavaro is bordered with numerous all-inclusive resorts, many with cool refreshing drinks served beach-side.

Punta Cana
Punta Cana beach is often referred to as the coconut coast due to its hundreds of swaying coconut palms scattered along the 30 miles of super fine white sand. This resort area is perhaps the DR's most popular vacation destination.

Punta Cana is outlined by a large concentration of all-inclusive resorts, each with their own garden of sun chairs and cabanas. However, despite the number of people who idle the day away here, the beach's size ensures visitors will never feel crowded. Those who don't want to spend their time simply baking in the sun can participate in an array of activities from beach volleyball to parasailing.

Playa Dominicus
The first beach in the Caribbean to have Blue Flag status (an eco-label showing high honors in a beach's commitment to sustainable development), Playa Dominicus is popular with scuba divers due to the presence of a large reef. Located near Bayahibe, Playa Dominicus is bordered by several all inclusive resorts

Playa Minitas

Playa Minitas is the private beach at the massive and luxurious Casa de Campo resort in La Romana. A variety of water sports are available at this exclusive stretch of sand as well as the resort's famous Minitas Beach pina colada served in a huge pineapple.

North Coast Region

It seems that each of the Dominican Republic's major regions has a nickname and the North Coast is no different. Featuring the popular towns of Puerto Plata, Cabarete and Sosua, the north coast has been referred to as the Amber Coast due to the prevalence of this semi-precious gem, the Discovery Coast thanks to Christopher Columbus discovery of the island of Hispaniola at Cape Isabela, and the Silver Coast, after Columbus named the area Puerto Plata or silver port because of the effect the sun made on the water as he approached.

Regardless of what visitor's call it, the north coast brings together some of the country's best features - lush jungle forests, rolling mountain ranges, ethereal blue waters and golden sand beaches. And it is because of these characteristics that this area is today considered the country's most versatile playground. Here vacationers can jump river beds on a mountain bike, fight the waves on a kiteboard, test their strength on a rock face or rub elbows with the rich and famous who come for the north coast's luxurious new accommodations. No matter what activity visitors choose to partake in, however, they'll find that everything here is done with legendary Dominican flair.

Cabarete

Over the past few years Cabarete has grown to achieve international fame, especially with a younger audience. The reason may be found on the town's beach, ranked as one of the world's top five kiteboarding and windsurfing destinations. So good are the conditions here, in fact, that Cabarete is regularly a stop in International competitions.

Cabarete offers more than just kiteboarding and windsurfing, however. Adventure sports enthusiasts come here for a range of activities including mountain biking, rock climbing, hiking, whitewater rafting and the like.

Given Cabarete's popularity with the younger set, it's no wonder that the town sports nightlife as varied as its daytime activities. Carretera 5, the town's main road, is jam packed with bars and dance clubs, many of which feature live music.

Playa Dorado

Widely known as the world's largest all-inclusive resort complex; Playa Dorada hosts 15 resorts, a mall, restaurants, golf and beaches. In fact, many guests spend their entire vacation within the complex walls.

Puerto Plata

With 200,000 residents, Puerto Plata is the largest city on the Dominican Republic's North Coast. The center of the town is called Old City and it is here that Puerto Plata's famed Victorian houses and narrow streets can be found.

While Puerto Plata itself isn't a top tourist attraction, vacationers who want a more cultural experience will enjoy visiting its quaint Parque Central which features a two-story Victorian gazebo. This area also features an array of eclectic bars and restaurants.

Sosua
By far one of the prettiest spots on the North Coast, Sosua is situated on a breathtaking Caribbean bay spotted with white sand beaches, rock formations and luxurious homes and resorts.

Featuring a mix of all-inclusive and luxury boutiques, the town offers a range of activities to fit any visitor. This once sleepy fishing village is now a top tourist destination as evidenced by the wealth of bars, restaurants and shops that line its streets. Despite this, Sosua has hung onto a small town charm that is all its own.

Here are the beaches on the North Coast region:

Cabarete
On the Dominican Republic's north coast, adventure seekers will fall in love with Cabarete. One of the top five kiteboarding and windsurfing beaches in the world, Cabarete's beach (often called Kite Beach) annually hosts an array of international championships. On any given day, visitors to the area will see the

sky filled with hundreds of colorful kites carrying amateur and pro riders through the surf.

Playa Cofresi
Just a few minutes west of Puerto Plata lays one of the most breathtaking beaches in the Dominican Republic named for the pirate Roberto Cofresi. While Playa Cofresi is wonderful for bathing in the sun, the waters provide excellent bodysurfing and boogie-boarding opportunities with its choppier waters. Two lodging options serve as the backdrop to the beach: Sun Village Resort & Spa and Hacienda Resort.

Playa Dorada
Located just east of Puerto Plata at the foot of the largest all-inclusive resort complex in the world, Playa Dorada is protected by reefs and features golf sand and warm waters. While anyone can drive into the Playa Dorada complex, non-guests have to pay for a day pass.

Playa Grande
At 1.5 miles long, Playa Grande, located near Luperon, is one of the longest beaches on the north coast. However, the beach is impressive not only for its size but also its breathtaking beauty. While the Occidental Allegro resort is now located at one end of the beach and food vendors sit at the other, the beach in between offers plenty of room to spread out.

Playa Punta Rucia
West of Puerto Plata and just off the beaten path, Playa Punta Rucia boasts white sand beaches and beautiful mountain views. Popular with snorkelers due to the presence of a large coral reef just off the shore, Playa Punta Rucia offers a small selection of restaurants/bars and a peaceful lagoon that is good for bird watching.

Playa Sosua
Located on a crescent-shaped bay, Playa Sosua is a postcard perfect beach. Featuring a backdrop of towering cliffs, the waters here are calm, clear and a deep shade of turquoise. Playa Sosua is perhaps one of the Caribbean's most popular beaches, which may explain the crowds. However, with so much to do - shopping or eating in Sosua, snorkeling or even taking a glass bottom boat tour - the crowds are worth the visit.

North East Coast

The Dominican Republic really does offer something for everyone. For those who dream of a one-on-one with Mother Nature, a visit to the Samana peninsula on the Northeast Coast is like pulling up a chair on her front porch.

Samana's beauty lies in her simplicity. Here, unspoiled beaches serve as a threshold to vibrant coral reefs while mountain waterfalls intersect lush rain forests. But while Samana is a top destination for eco-tourists and naturalists, some come to this off the beaten path peninsula to interact with humpback whales. After all, Samana is home to one of the largest and best breeding grounds in the world for this elusive mammal.

But while Samana's beauty is the stuff of legends, its history is fodder fit for a fairytale. Columbus stopped here on his discovery of the New World but the area didn't become populated until late in 1756 when people began migrating from the Canary Islands. Soon Samana became a lair for pirates who pillaged passing ships. What followed was a short ownership by Napolean Bonaparte and later, settlement by freed American slaves.

All this history and meshing of cultures has left Samana as one of the most impressive melting pots in the Dominican Republic. Americanos, descendents of the African-American inhabitants, mix with Europeans from France, Spain and Italy. Not only do people here *look* different from their Dominican brethren, but the food and even the language has a twist all its own.

Las Galeras

At the tip of Samana peninsula, close to world-famous Playa Rincon, lies the town of Las Galeras. This small fishing village has experienced a boom in the past few years with the addition of a large all-inclusive resort (Casa Marina Bay) and several smaller hotels. However, because of its remote location, Las Galeras has been able to maintain its serene nature. So idyllic is this town that it is a popular honeymoon destination for those couples who want a true escape to paradise.

The main attraction in Las Galeras is the beach found at the end of the town's main road. Here visitors can meet locals who gather at the beach's food kiosks. Hotels can give information on catching the ferry to Playa Rincon or beachfront horseback riding, a particular favorite of tourists to the area.

Samana

The town of Samana is located on the southern side of the peninsula along Samana Bay. It's a popular base for tourists who plan to participate in whale watching excursions or day trips to Cayo Levantado, both of which leave from the town's port. Samana's Malecon, or beachfront strip, is the center of activity and features outdoor cafes and small shops.

Samana is heavily populated by Americanos, descendents of freed American slaves. Because of this the town holds a series of annual harvest festivals, a tradition dating back to the Yam and Rice festivals of West Africa. These lively events are held on Fridays from late August through the end of October at Samana churches.

Las Terrenas

Perhaps the most popular destination on the peninsula is the resort town of Las Terrenas. Run primarily by French expats, Las Terrenas offers good variety of accommodations, ranging from all-inclusives to comfortable boutiques.

Visitors to Las Terrenas have no shortage of things to do. The town features several small malls, a wide variety of restaurants and even discos. Despite this, the highlight of a visit to Las Terrenas is the beach.

Here are the beaches located on the Samana Peninsula:

Cayo Levantado
Cayo Levantado is a small island located a few miles offshore from the town of Samana. Because it gets busy, it is recommended that visitors take the ferry early. It departs from the main port in Samana. On the opposite side of the island, smaller beaches are less frequented.

Las Terrenas

Located on the north coast of the Samana peninsula, Las Terrenas beach stretches one mile on either side of the town. Speckled with coconut palms, it's the perfect destination in which to enjoy a mix of sand, surf and shade. Casual restaurants are plentiful here, many of which are owned by expats from Europe (especially France) and North America.

Playa Bonita
A quiet eight mile beach located on the north side of Samana peninsula, Playa Bonita looks like something out of a movie set. Featuring white sand beach and clear turquoise waters (see a pattern here?), the area is framed by a few beach houses that only add to its charm.

Playa Las Flechas
Continuing the Spanish lesson, Playa Las Flechas translates to Beach of the Arrows. Legend has it this beach, located on the southeast tip of Samana peninsula, is named after a battle between Christopher Columbus and the Taino Indians, who occupied the land. A fairly quiet destination, Playa Las Flechas looks out onto Cayo Levantado.

Playa Rincon
Conde Nast Traveler ranked this beach as one of the world's 10 best. It's so splendid, in fact, that many Dominicans refer to it as the most beautiful on the island. Over three miles long, Playa Rincon is surrounded by coconut palms and almond trees, not to mention a 2,000 foot mountain on one end. Again, the best way to get to this isolated beach is by boat; a ride that is definitely worth it. (Boat rides are available from Las Galeras.)

South Central Region

While the Dominican Republic's coasts provide relaxation at every turn, Santo Domingo and the South Central Region are all hustle and bustle. With just over three million people, Santo Domingo serves as the Caribbean's most diverse destination and, arguably, the most vibrant. The city itself displays contrasts at every turn. Contemporary hotels sit on ancient cobblestone streets, luxury cars parked beside well-worn scooters, and eclectic cuisine at hip restaurants is served next to street vendors serving traditional Dominican fare.

As the oldest city in the New World, Santo Domingo features the first cathedral, first university and first hospital of the Americas. In fact, visitors often note that the well-preserved Zona Colonial makes them feel as though they've been transported in time.

Despite all this history, Santo Domingo is quite modern and very continental. The city's restaurants offer just about any cuisine in the world, boutiques and major chain retailers from the U.S. and Europe have set-up shops, and a wealth of museums, galleries and theaters ensure countless cultural events.

Boca Chica and Jaun Dolio

Boca Chica
Conveniently located near Santo Domingo's airport, Boca Chica is a resort town bustling with activity. The beach is actually a reef-protected lagoon characterized by powdery sand and turquoise waters. And because of its conditions - calm, warm waters - the area is a popular destination for Santo Domingo residents and their children on the weekends.

Considered a shopping beach, vendors set-up shop up and down the main street that runs parallel to the beach. Visitors, many of whom come from the wide array of the hotels and resorts in the area, can buy everything from jewelry and artwork to food and drinks.

Hotels and resorts fitting any budget are located here, as well as an array of nightlife and restaurants.

Juan Dolio
Located halfway between Santo Domingo and La Romana, Juan Dolio is a perfect escape for couples and families. While the town is calm and peaceful, excitement is only minutes away in the form of an excursion to La Romana or Santo Domingo. Other excursions include scuba diving, a baseball game at San Pedro Tetelo Vargas stadium, or one of the many other day trips available from tour operators.

Here are the beaches in the South Central Region:

Boca Chica
The beach most popular with Santo Domingo residents, Boca Chica is busy and loaded with food stands and entrepreneurial Dominicans selling everything from food to personal tours. Despite this, the waters off the shore are shallow and therefore kid-friendly.

Playa Juan Dolio
While the waters at Playa Juan Dolio are not as ideal for swimming as neighboring Boca Chica, the beach is not as busy. Restaurants, bars and resorts line the beach and provide all-day entertainment.

Playa Guayacanes
Nestled between Juan Dolio and Boca Chica, this sandy beach is a local favorite for boogie-boarding.

South West Coast

If the Dominican Republic has a well-kept secret, the western region of the country is it. Essentially, this region includes the area west of Santo Domingo, and it is still an undiscovered territory by many tourists. Visitors seeking areas less traveled would be wise to experience this peaceful region before it becomes a popular destination. The farthest part of the region is only about a three hour drive from Santo Domingo or Santiago airports.

Although the Dominican Republic provides a change of scenery at just about every turn, this region is the most diverse ecologically. Two salt water lakes, one being the largest in the Caribbean, provide a haven for massive populations of birds and reptiles. And while some sections of the area are mountain rainforest, other parts are pine forest and arid desert.

Barahona

Just a three hour drive west of Santo Domingo lies the remote, relaxed, and remarkable town of Barahona. Founded in 1802, the region became a recognized fishing town and agricultural city famous for its large plantains and vast collection of coffee and sugar.

However, the town itself is not what draws people to this natural environment. Here, spectacular cliffs make the ultimate backdrop to the many secluded beaches and streams.

The people of Barahona are warm and inviting and its coastlines are calm and unspoiled.

Amongst the more notable characteristics of Barahona are the very rural, modest surroundings. Besides the little disco clubs scattered throughout the area, there is nothing glitzy about the southwest region. Here, locals dwell in the famous "tejemani" style of houses, built with intertwining sticks and branches. Perhaps it is for the seclusion and slow-pace that visitors are so eager to return. The wealth of Barahona lies not in individual belongings, but the beauty and heart of the people and surroundings.

San Cristobal

The first major city west of Santo Domingo, San Cristobal is considered by many as a small version of the capital. The city of 170,000 thrives on its sugar cane mills and herb fields. Its arid ground and mountain background serve as a gateway to the Wild West. Just south of San Cristobal is the village of Nigua where 16th-century and 18th-century ruins of sugar mills can be explored.

For a more Indiana Jones-like experience, head north from San Cristobal. The Cuevas de Borbon is a series of 40 connecting caves including the Cuevas de El Pomier, a particular section that has more than 5,000 petroglyphs and several thousand Amerindian wall paintings. Bring a flashlight to spot the thousands of bats that make the cave their home.

Pedernales

This small fishing village serves as a portal to several different areas and adventures. Two of the country's major national parks, Parque Nacional Jaragua to the southwest and Parque Nacional Sierra de Bahoruco to the north serve as borders making the village an excellent base camp for hikers. Pedernales also provides easy access for those visitors wishing to explore Haiti, whose border is just to the west.

Two rarely visited islands are just a boat ride away from the village: Alto Velo and Isla Beata. The rocky, scrub-brush environment of Isla Beata sets the scene for Taino caves which features enough rock art to fill a coffee table book. Alto Velo has been referred to as a giant stone sailboat protruding out of the water. The high rocky land of this small island provides habitat for the world's smallest reptile, the dwarf gecko measuring less than two centimeters across, or the size of a Dominican peso coin.

Here is a list of the South West Beaches:

Playa Pedernales
Located near the Haitian border, this beach is close to the fishing village of Pedernales. While the beach is quite peaceful during the day, at night it comes alive with small fishing boats returning to shore.

San Rafael
Located south of Barahona, the beach at San Rafael is a hot spot for local Dominicans. Here visitors will find the best of both worlds – a strong ocean surf but also a natural swimming pool formed by a waterfall descending from the nearby mountains. A manmade barrier allows the water from the pool to gently pour into the ocean.

Choosing the region you would like to invest in

The first thing that you need to decide when you choosing a region to invest in is; what do you want out of this investment?

In a later chapter we will discuss the different types of real estate that can be owned such as villas, land, condos, commercial, hotels, and so on. In this section I will try to persuade you to think about why you are investing in the DR. The reason for your investment will play a huge part in your decision on where to invest.

Questions you should ask yourself:

1. Am I looking for a vacation or retirement home that I plan on spending a lot of time at?

If the answer to this question is yes, then the region you choose to invest in must also be one where you can see your self living. Are you the type of person who needs access to the latest luxuries? Or do you prefer to live off the beaten path? Do you want to be around mostly locals or other expatriates? Do you want to be a pioneer in an up and coming area or would you prefer to dwell in an already established one? Are you a city person or a beach person?

As you can see, if you are planning to spend a lot of time at your purchase then you need to figure out exactly what you want. Once you know what you want it will be a lot easier to find it.

2. Am I looking to own this real estate for a short term gain, or am I looking to see it appreciate over a number of years?

If you are looking for a short term gain then you will most likely be looking for an area that is already semi established and on the brink of an immediate growth spurt. If you are looking to own the real estate for a number of years then you have the option of purchasing in an area that has not yet been developed.

3. Am I looking to make an immediate cash flow on the investment?

If you are purchasing this property with the intention of immediately renting it out in hopes of covering your monthly expenses and making a cash flow then you need to choose a region that has rent producing potential.

If you are purchasing in hopes of renting to tourists at a premium then you need to purchase in a tourist area such as Cabarete, Punta Cana, or Las Terrenas.

If you are looking to rent it out monthly to locals then you are probably better off investing in a city where more of the residents are working class such as Santa Domingo or Santiago.

4. How much can I really afford to spend on this investment?

This is an important question you must ask yourself. And you must be truthful with yourself. Prices vary throughout the island. For instance, if you are looking for an ocean front condo and have a budget of under $100,000 than Punta Cana may not be an option for you.

If you are looking for land the prices range from $2 a square foot to $200 a square foot depending on the region, the beach, the development complex and so on.

There really is no point wasting your time looking in areas that are out of your price range. The more you know the market the easier it will be to know where your target area should be.

So in summary, when deciding on which area you want to invest in, it is important to really ask your self these important questions:

1. Am I looking for a vacation or retirement home that I plan on spending a lot of time at?
2. Am I looking to own this real estate for a short term gain, or am I looking to see it appreciate over a number of years?
3. Am I looking to make an immediate cash flow on the investment?
4. How much can I really afford to spend on this investment?

You are the only one who can answer these questions. Before you proceed with your investment you must decide exactly what you want out of it. Because in the Dominican Republic it is all available. And if you have a clear picture of what you want, you will surely find it.

Chapter 3

Evaluating the different types of real estate

OK, you have finally chosen an area that you would like to purchase some property in. Or at least you have narrowed it down to a couple specific locations. The next step, which may actually narrow the location down further, is to decide exactly what kind of investment you would like to put your money in.

Start by deciding why you're buying the real estate. Think of all real estate falling into a continuum with one end being your personal residence and the other end being pure investment. For your personal residence, many factors influence what you buy, but the most important one is whether you enjoy spending time at the property. On the pure investment end, again there are many factors, including the projected return, your overall diversification strategy, and how the investment fits into your portfolio.

Most people decide to invest in an area with very little knowledge of exactly what they want. They are so happy to finally have made the decision on where to invest that they don't realize that there are still other decisions to be made. Major decisions!

If you answered the crucial question that I listed in Chapter 2 you will have an easier time deciding what kind of property to purchase. If you haven't answered the questions take the time right now to answer them. I've left space for you to write your answer out as it may be helpful to continually remind yourself of the answers as you read about each investment vehicle.

1. Am I looking for a vacation or retirement home that I plan on spending a lot of time at?

_____

2. Am I looking to own this real estate for a short term gain, or am I looking to see it appreciate over a number of years?

_____

3. Am I looking to make an immediate cash flow on the investment?

_____

4. How much can I really afford to spend on this investment?

_____

The answers to these questions should help shape your plan. But there are even more questions that you need to ask yourself when deciding what type of property you are going to purchase.

More questions you should ask yourself

1. How much risk am I willing to take?

_____

This is an important question when deciding what kind of property to invest in. Although all investments carry some type of risk, some are by nature riskier then others. If you are purchasing land in area that has yet to build roads or have electricity, the investment would be considered just a tad riskier then purchasing a condo in a well established beach town. Of course there is the old saying "The greater the risk, the greater the reward."

2. How active do I want to be in managing and maintaining your investment?

_____

Are you purchasing this property with the plan of treating it like a stock, and just sitting on it for ten or fifteen years, without thinking about it? If that's the case then land would be a much better choice then say a small hotel.

Although there are damn good management companies in the Dominican Republic there is still much that needs to be taken care of on a weekly basis when dealing with a hotel, condo, or villa. It is important to be aware of what your responsibilities will be as owner of the property.

3. How quickly do I want to be able to liquidate my investment if a time comes where I need to cash out?

This is something that you absolutely must think about. While you may have a concrete plan on how long you want to own the property for (possibly forever) you can never predict the future. There may come a time when you are forced to sell. In evaluating the different types of properties you must take into consideration which ones are the most easily liquidated and which ones may be harder to sell in a time of crisis.

Much of this decision depends on what the rest of your investment portfolio looks like. If you have a big diversity in your portfolio and have other assets that can be sold easily for cash then this question is not as important as if it is your only investment, and the only asset you can sell for cash in a time of need.

4. Do I plan on using bank financing for the purchase of the property in the Dominican Republic?

The reason that you must ask your self this question before deciding what kind of investment you are going to make is because banks are very fussy with their guidelines for international property mortgages.

For instance, the loan program that we use most often here in New Jersey only offers financing for condos and houses. No matter how much the buyer is willing to put down they will not lend on land, new construction, or commercial buildings.

So if you are planning on using a bank for financing you must find out what their guidelines are. You must find out what kind of properties they are willing to finance.

The different types of real estate

Once you have answered the above questions you can now take a look at each of the different types of real estate and have a better idea of how well it would fit into your investment plan.

Obviously all real estate is different. Even once I've narrowed the types down to the six types I am going to talk about in this chapter, there are many subtypes and alterations available within. That is one of the beauties of real estate; if you look hard enough it is always possible to get something tailored to your exact needs.

Condos

I am going to start this section talking about condos because they are the simplest real estate investment available.

The reason that I make this claim is for a variety of reason that I will go over below.

Pros

One of the things that make condos a simple and easy investment is the amount of them available on the market. There are thousands of condos available at all times throughout the Dominican Republic. This means that you will always have a large selection to choose from.

The large selection of condos also allows you to get a good grasp of what they are going for in each particular region. It is easier to establish a market value for something that has already sold several other units in the complex. It is much harder to get a grasp on the market value of a villa or hotel which may be unique to its area.

Another reason that makes condos a simple easy investment is the fact that they are probably one of the easier investments to acquire bank financing for. Because they are so plentiful and much easier to appraise then a villa or hotel, banks seem to feel more confident lending money for their purchase.

Along with the availability of bank financing is the fact that they are usually less expensive to purchase than a house, villa, or hotel. The fact that they are less expensive means there is also a bigger turnover ratio and in the right market will be easier to find a buyer.

Condos usually are less management intensive then a villa or hotel. This is because most condos have an on sight management company that handles much of the day to day responsibilities of the property such as landscape upkeep, pool maintenance, security issues, house keeping, and the payment of all utilities. This is because most condos have a monthly fee that will incorporate all of these charges. For many people this is easier than having to hire your own personal pool man, landscaper, and security guards.

Condos are usually pretty easy to rent. Because condos are often run by management companies many times you will have the option of them renting the condo for you for a small fee. This is especially attractive for the investor who doesn't want to have to deal with finding renters, answering questions, and so on.

The condo complexes are usually filled with other foreigners who have made their way to the Dominican Republic. This is more important for those investors who plan on spending a lot of time at their investment. Because most of the condo complexes were built with the intention of selling to foreigners it is a good place to meet other ex patriots and retirees living in the area. These people will often have helpful hints about the area and will often become friends of yours. Even if the owner doesn't reside in the condo often, chances are the people renting the condo will be tourists as well. This gives you a chance to play host and send them in the right direction on their trip. If you help make their experience enjoyable these same people may wind up renting your condo the next time they are down.

Cons

The liquidation of a condo is relatively easy. But problems can arise if too many people are trying to sell units in the same complex at the same time. As with anything when then supply exceeds the demand the prices tend to drop. Unfortunately for condo owners the prices of condos are the first to drop in any declining real estate market. With so many condos out there you also have less control over the going rate as you would if you owned, say, a villa.

Many people like to have complete control over their investments. The fact that there are condo associations and management companies involved sometimes leaves owners feeling like it is not entirely their own investment. The owner does not have the final say that one would have if they were owner of a house. This is the same for condo owners in the United States where the condo associations play a role in the decision making.

The appreciation of a condo is usually not as significant as the appreciation of raw land or a house built on a large portion of land. This is particularly true of beach front land. I am in no way saying that your condo can't double or even triple in value. When you own a condo you don't really own the land that it is on. Often in a thriving market the land becomes worth more then the real estate. Owners of small houses on large portions of land can take advantage of this and sell out of a huge profit to someone looking to build on the land. Condo owners do not have that option.

How much do condos go for?

As with any real estate the price of condos vary greatly depending on many factors. The main three main factors as always are; location, location, location.

With out a doubt the most expensive properties are those located on the beach with ocean views. Because there is always a lot less beachfront properties available the prices tend to be much much higher than something very similar on the other side of the street.

You must really consider how important owning beach front property is to you. If you plan on visiting the condo often is it something you feel you need to enjoy your stay there?

Often times when you are browsing web pages you will see property advertised as beach front property for like $70,000- $80,000. This is what we call in the real estate business the bait and switch. I made that mistake early on by seeing these prices without seeing the actual condos and assuming that a beach front condo can be purchased in the Dominican Republic for around that cost. This is usually not the case. Owners of these condos tend to be very liberal in their definition of beach front.

True beach front condos can seldom be found for under $100,000 anywhere in the commercialized Dominican Republic. As new areas are being developed if you get in during an early phase of new construction it may be possible to nab one for less. But if you looking for a condo in Cabarete, Sosua, Boca Chica, Punta Cana, or Samana, you are more than likely going to pay over $100,000. And at this price you still may have a short walk to the actual beach.

There are condos available on the less desirable beaches at reduced rates. These include beaches filled with rocks and little sand, sections of beaches that are usually filled with boats or kite surfers. If having an ocean view is more important then a beach to actually lay down for a tan on, then one of these condos may be perfect for you. With a helpful realtor it is still possible to acquire one of these condos for less than $100,000 in the main investment areas.

Another factor in the cost of a condo is how many bedrooms it has. Here is a sample of pricing for ocean front condos in Cabarete. These are new condos with all the amenities located in the heart of Cabarete near all the restaurants and shops.

Oceanfront studios from $104,000
Oceanfront two bedroom apartments from $235,000
Oceanfront three bedroom apartments from $399,000

As you can see the prices vary considerably depending on the amount of bedrooms it has. You must consider how many bedrooms you need for your personal use if you plan on visiting it frequently. You must also keep in mind the rental price disparities for studios, two bedrooms, and three bedrooms. All though the price may be significantly higher for more bedrooms, sometimes the difference in the rent you can charge make up for the higher price.

In general condos in the Dominican Republic can be purchased from around $30,000 to upwards of $500,000 depending on location, size, and luxuries.

If you are purchasing the condo as a vacation home for you and your family then what is really important is what suits your needs. If you are purchasing this condo in hopes of seeing some immediate appreciation the condos in the $100,000 range are the ones I believe have the most room to grow. The thirty and forty thousand dollar condos are generally located in a less secure part of town or they are located in an old run down complex. These condos have potentially for value growth if outside factors come into play. If a seedy neighborhood has some money dumped in then there is a chance that all the real estate located within it will raise in value. There is also the possibility of a new management team taking over and renovating an old condo complex. If you get into one of the units before the renovation you can stand to profit.

Investing in a condo in a bad neighborhood or a run down complex is more speculating. It is like investing in a penny stock. Unless you have some serious inside information from a reliable source more than likely the area will not be changing for a long time. If you are the speculating type I would suggest reading the next section on investing in land. It is a much safer form of speculation as the value of land rarely decreases.

Land

Types of Land

Although I have to assume that most people purchasing this book are looking more for the chance to own close to the ocean. For the purpose of this section I will talk about all the possibilities when it comes to land. With the relatively low cost of land throughout the Dominican there is potential to make a nice profit no matter where you purchase if you understand the dynamics of land ownership.

Though land can be categorized and subcategorized probably infinitely, for the purpose of this discussion, I divide land into rural, exurban, suburban, and beach front.

Rural
In the rural land category, I include farmland (which the DR has plenty of) ranchland, tree farms, timberlands, and the like. As population and industrial centers proliferate worldwide, and the developing areas encroach on nearby rural acreage, that land obviously becomes more valuable, making this a potentially high-return investment.

Obviously, land that is part of an income-producing property helps generate more income (and value) than farmland. Although rural unimproved land produces some income, the return is miniscule relative to farmland's value.

The price of land takes into account its long term irreplaceability and future appreciation in both crop prices and land value.

Rural land carries with it both short and long term value:

Short term. Values fluctuate in relationship to what the land can produce and the value of the production. For example, if the price of wheat goes up, the value of wheat producing farmland also rises.

Long term. In general, the same factors influencing other long-term investments affect land values in the long run: irreplaceability, population growth, inflation, and the related demand for food and other goods.

Pros

Usually, rural land investments enjoy long-term appreciation due to inflation and nearby population center expansion.

Rural land investments offer intangible benefits such as pride and satisfaction of owning a farm. For those who truly "love the land."

Rural land is irreplaceable.

Cons

Relatively large amounts of money have to be tied up for a long period of time. Farms usually have limited annual cash return on amounts invested.

Short term income and land values are subject to the quantity of, and demand for, the crops produced.

Although a farm can be managed from oversees with the help of a good team, there are numerous problems that can occur that you may have to deal with.

Investment potential for the novice

This type of investment is not for the novice investor with limited funds, because immediate cash flow return is relatively low, and if the land lays idle, there may be more out of pocket costs such as insurance, utilities, and upkeep.

ExUrban Land

As the suburbs mature and grow, and themselves become urban, the exurbs- that is, land just beyond the outskirts of the suburbs- becomes the new suburbs. Before this takes place, however, exurban land is usually considered rural, as described in the previous section. Rural land becomes exurban when it is considered to be within reasonable commuting distance from the inner city, usually approximately 50-100 miles away. The only cities where this land is of any importance is outside of Santo Domingo and Santiago, and to a lesser extent Puerto Plata.

Advantages

Owners usually report intangible pleasures of living and managing "country places" especially when they are raising families.

The profit potential from future development of exurban land, especially in these times of widening city circumferences, is enticing.
You can buy a mini-estate of 5 to 10 acres at a commutable distance from an urban center, which has tremendous potential to sell to the wealthy Dominicans.

Disadvantages

You tie up capital in a non income producing investment.
You have to pay of out of pocket costs yourself.
You lack the city advantages of hospitals, schools, and professional services.

Investment potential for the novice

I would not heavily recommend exurban land for the novice investor with limited funds, because the money will be tied up for long periods without generating any cash flow. In addition the owner will have to pay real estate taxes (if the government feels like collecting) insurance, and other expenses without the benefit of offsetting income.

Suburban land

Dominican Republic doesn't have much of what we call in the United States suburban land. Outside of the major cities there are some areas that as close to the term as you will find in the Dominican Republic. The opportunity for growth in suburban real estate in the Dominican Republic depends heavily on the countries economic future. If the middle class population in the DR can grow then there is money to be made. I will also include all land in the beach communities that is not beach front.

Pros

Purchasing strategically placed land for a reasonable price can be an excellent long term investment.
Undeveloped land does not require extensive management and therefore can be taken care of easily.
If there is a home on the land, you get the benefits of home ownership as well.

Cons

The converse of the first advantage is the out of pocket carrying cost- taxes, insurance, and the like- must be paid because land does not produce income. You interest on the cash invested- though hopefully you will make it up when the price of the land appreciates.
If you insist on leveraging land investments you will also have to make loan payments, as no off setting income is produced.

Investment potential for the novice
Buying a home with, say, a 5-acre tract of land in a rapidly growing area can provide the benefits of semirural land and a residence while waiting for appreciation. But I do not recommend that new, small investors with limited funds speculate in the ownership of exurban land, as it ties up too much money that could be invested for more immediate returns.

Beach Front Land

Ah… One of reasons that you probably picked up this book. Dominican Republic is filled with beach front land. Some of it is has been developed but most stretches of beach still lie upon barren land.

Historically beach front land is a commodity. Like gold, silver, and oil, only so much of it exists on this earth, and it is something that seems to always be in high demand. Something about being near the ocean has captivated humans for centuries. And it will continue to captivate humans for centuries.

The beaches at all the resort/vacation areas of the Dominican Republic have pretty much been developed. There are still small lots of land here and there, but the prices of these lots reflect the fact that roadways, electricity, and commerce has already been instituted in the area. This is not to say that this property will not continue to see increases in its value. Unlike the other sectors of land, beach front is not so much affected by the Dominican economy as it is the world economy, since foreigners generally are the ones who purchase this land.

There are plenty of areas right outside the major resort/vacation areas that are prime for the taking. The price of land right outside these areas can be as much as twenty to thirty dollars per sq meter cheaper. For instance land in Samana goes from roughly $20 per sq down to $6 or $7 per sq meter. Land in more developed regions like Sosua can range from $50 per sq meter to $300 per sq meter. Beach Available on the Cost of Punta Cana Caribbean Sea, Prices ranging from US$ 25-190 per square meters. As you can see there are large fluctuations in prices even in the same area.

Short term
If you are looking to invest for the short term, than your goal would be to purchase a nice piece of beach property in an already developed region. You could make your money on your investment by building a villa, condo complex, or hotel and selling it at a nice profit.

If you are a savvy investor or have some reliable connections down there you can purchase land that other builders have their eyes on and purchase the land only to flip it over to them shortly after for a nice profit.

Long Term

If you are looking to invest for the long term (3 or more years) than a good investment would be the up and coming areas right outside the already established ones. For instance land less than an hour outside of Sosua goes for a third of its price. How long do you think it will take for that area to become developed? That is your exit strategy. If you are good at predicting these things or can build a team around you who is good at predicting these things you can become a millionaire fairly easily.

Pros

Purchasing beach front land is like making an investment in gold. Through different economic cycles it may have its ups and down but in the long run it will always see an increase in value as it is a commodity that lessens in supply every year.

Undeveloped land does not require extensive management and therefore can be taken care of easily.

You can build a home on the land and have the benefits of owning a home near the ocean. You also have the potential to rent the home out each month to cover carrying costs of the land.

Cons

The converse of the second advantage is the out of pocket carrying cost- taxes, insurance, and the like- must be paid because land does not produce income.

Your interest on the cash invested- though hopefully you will make it up when the price of the land appreciates.

If you insist on leveraging land investments you will also have to make loan payments, as no off setting income is produced.

Investment potential for the novice

Purchasing beach front land is a much better investment than the other types of land talked about in this section. While I don't think it is necessarily the best place to begin your investment in the Dominican Republic, with the help of some good real estate professionals familiar with the different sections of beaches it is a pretty sturdy investment. The major drawback on owning solely raw land is that not only do you not have any income to offset the carrying costs; you also do not get to enjoy your investment as you would a condo, house, or small hotel.

Houses and Villas

For the purpose of this book I am only going to talk about houses and villas located within walking distance of a beach. Although there are some sections of the Dominican Republic that have middle and upper class neighborhoods these homes are usually occupied by locals and unless you are planning on moving to the Dominican Republic they do not make much sense as investments.

Villas located in vacation/resort areas are a different story. These homes have usually been designed by foreigners with the intention of selling to foreigners. They vary from individual villas on the beach to villas located within a gated community such as the Sea Horse Ranch is Sosua. They can be little two bedroom beach bungalows or they can be giant 12 bedroom mansions. If you are designing and having it built is can literally be anything that you want.

Pros

One of the most basic advantages of purchasing a villa is the fact that you get all the benefits of owning a vacation home. In the Dominican Republic you can pay less for a custom designed house near the beach as you would for a small ranch twenty minutes or more from the beach in most places in the United States.

Villas come in all shapes and sizes so it is easy to find one that suits your needs directly. If you own a piece of land you can hire an architect to design the home of your dreams.

There will always be people with money. These people tend to like to own property near the beach. Many of these people prefer the seclusion of villa ownership to more community like condo. This means that there will always be a market for your villa when you decide to sell.

Villas usually sit on a decent amount of land. As the value of land appreciates so does the value of all construction that sits on it. Purchasing a preexisting villa is a great way to purchase land. I look at it like buying land with a bonus.

Like condos, villas offer the potential of rental income to offset the carrying costs of the property. Many families prefer the privacy of renting a villa to staying in a hotel on their vacations. I've been renting villas whenever I go on vacation for years for the sole reason that I like night swimming, and that is not allowed in most hotels. Villas offer a nice rental income. Most villas start at over $1,000 a week to rent. Some villas charge five to ten thousand a week. And they get it!!! I'm not saying that your villa will be rented out 52 weeks a year, but you definitely will receive some income to offset the costs of maintaining the villa.

Cons

One of the major drawbacks of a villa as an initial investment is the price. Although prices can fluctuate from village to village depending on how developed the area is, a modest sized villa in a good part of town will run at least $200k. Villas on the water or extremely close to the water will probably run you $400k or more. The high price doesn't necessarily mean it's a bad investment, it just means that there is more capital needed to get involved with it.

The amount of capital you need extends to the carrying costs of maintaining the villa. If you don't have rental income supplementing the costs every month they can start to really add up. These costs include but are not limited to:

groundkeeper, pool cleaner, maid, security guards, taxes, insurance, mortgage payments, and management fees.

The management of a villa is more intensive than a condo. As stated above; you will have to hire a groundskeeper, pool cleaner, security guards, maids, and management. Of course this all depends on your personal preference and needs. If you are only using the villa as your vacation home you can skip some of the above, but if you plan on renting the villa they are all a must. I will go more into management of investments in a later chapter.

The high price tag limits the amount of potential purchasers for your villa. It is easier to find someone looking to spend $100k than it is to find someone looking to spend $400k.

If you are looking to invest in more than one property you are tying up a lot of money and resources on this one property. With the cost of purchasing and maintaining a villa you can purchase and maintain several condos in different locations throughout the island. This gives you a chance to diversify rather than putting all your eggs in one basket.

Investment potential for the novice

This is a hard one to determine. Only you can answer this as I don't know your personal financial status. If money is not an issue, than there is definitely investment potential. Although the thought of maintaining a villa may seem a bit intimidating there are many management teams in the Dominican Republic who, for a fee, will take care of most of those aspects.

There is definitely potential for appreciation when purchasing a villa. I've met many people down there who've seen their villa double in value in only a few years. I can't guarantee this will happen to you, but the potential does exist.

While this may not be as simple an investment as a condo, I do believe that there is potential for a novice, assuming he has the capital to purchase and maintain the villa.

Small hotel or Bed and Breakfast

Have you always dreamed about owning your own little hotel in the sun? You may have actually dreamed about moving there to run it. I think that is a dream that everyone has had at some point in their life. The Dominican Republic is the perfect place to make that dream a reality.

For the scope of this section I am only going to talk about purchasing a small hotel (less than 20 rooms) or a bed and breakfast. There are opportunities to build, buy, and manage much larger hotels and resorts in the Dominican Republic but that goes beyond the scope of this book.

I also want to remind everyone reading this that sometimes an investment is not so much about what kind of return you make on your money as it is fulfilling a lifelong dream. Owning a small hotel on a Caribbean island has more intangible benefits than I could fit in this book. For a retiring workaholic it may just be the stress reducer that prolongs his life ten years... For another it may be the joy that brings them out of depression. My point with these examples is just to remind you that sometimes the value of an investment goes beyond ROI and capital gains and the like.

On my last trip to the Dominican Republic on a car ride from Sosua to Samana I stopped at a small hotel called "Gringo Beach" along the way. It looked like something straight out of Fiji with the beach front huts and secluded privacy perfect for the honeymooning couple. I met with the owners, a couple of guys from Belgium and can safely say I've met few people as happy and content as they were. They said that the inn is not going to make them millionaires but it pays the bills and allows them to live the life they dreamed. Is that not priceless?

With that being said let's look at some of the pros and cons of purchasing a small hotel in the Caribbean.

Pros

If you plan on moving down to the Dominican and running the hotel yourself it is a chance to live a life that most people daydream about on a daily basis. You get the self satisfaction of knowing, win or lose, that you lived your dream. Not many people on this earth can say that. Like I said above the list of benefits of doing this is endless, but here are just a few: You will have a chance to meet people from all over the world. The relaxing Caribbean lifestyle is good for the mind, heart, and soul. You will have a place for your friends and family to stay when they come and visit.

A well run and properly managed small hotel in the right location has the potential to bring in a lot of money. How to run a small hotel is beyond the scope of this book, but the difference between good and bad management could mean the difference between a gold mine, and a money pit.

Since you are primarily catering to tourists you will be charging rates accordingly. How well your hotel does depends on your ability to successfully market your hotel to travel agencies who will push their clients there. There is unlimited potential for a savvy businessman to make it big with a small hotel.

Cons

The unlimited potential to make it big heavily depends on how well of a businessman you are. There are many aspects to running a hotel such as; marketing, management, upkeep, accounting, and sales. If you want to be successful you need to be able to create a team of people around you that can successfully accomplish all these things. This is not as easy as it sounds.

You will most likely be hiring mainly Dominicans and Haitians. This requires you to speak and understand some Spanish. Is it possible to run a hotel in the Dominican Republic and not speak Spanish? I am sure it has been done. But without a grasp of the language your job will be ten times harder.

You will also need extensive knowledge in local laws, tax implication, labor laws, and the like. There is much more research involved in opening a hotel than simply purchasing a condo or villa to rent out.

Hotels are not that liquid of an investment. Because at any given moment there are only so many people looking to open a small hotel compared to the amount of people looking to purchase a villa or condo, you may have difficulty selling your investment. If the hotel is not bringing in any income or has been closed down for a bit it may be even harder to sell. This could cause a huge problem for those who need to cash out quickly.

The startup cost of a hotel is much larger than most other real estate investments. Although in some parts of the Dominican a small hotel can be purchased for $400k or so, in the resort/vacation areas most these will be closer the $1,000,000 mark. Most investors without a prior history of successful hotel management will have trouble obtaining bank financing for this kind of a project.

The monthly cost involved with running a hotel can be huge. You will be employing quite a few people, and these people will be getting paid regardless of whether or not your hotel is bringing you in any money. In the beginning months before you have the chance to establish yourself you may struggle to find people to stay at your hotel. During these times you will still be paying all of your out of pocket costs such as; management fees, upkeep fees, taxes, finance payments (if any), marketing costs, and electric and gas charges.

If you plan on managing it from abroad you have to be extremely careful with whom you trust to run the place. While there are quite a few good management companies and employees in the Dominican Republic, there are just as many dishonest crooks that prey on unsuspecting foreigners. If your business lands in the wrong people's hands you can experience a quick downfall.

Investment potential for the novice

While I would never deliberately crush someone's dream of moving to the Dominican Republic to run a small hotel, I would strongly advise them to severely research what it takes to do so.

Running a hotel is not the most ideal investment for the novice. It takes a lot more time and energy than any of the previously talked about investments. It also takes a lot more up front money and much more capital to sustain it through its growth periods.

I would only recommend purchasing a small hotel to someone with previous experience with this kind of profession. I would also only recommend it to someone who has sufficient capital to withstand the potential loss involved.

Overall, I think that opening a small hotel is not safest or easiest investment for the novice.

New Construction

In the real estate boom that occurred in the United States from the turn of the millennium through the next five or six years one of the surefire ways to see instant appreciation was to purchase real estate during the construction phase.

During the construction of condos and townhouses many developers begin selling off units in the early phases to help with the financing of these properties. In a "hot" market the price of these condos and townhouses can increase 10-20% before they are even completed. In situations like this much money is made by speculators who purchase contracts to buy the properties, and then sell the contracts for a profit immediately after closing on the condo or townhouse.

In any booming market this is a game that investors and speculators play often. There is greater risk in purchasing during the early phase of a project which enables the purchaser to buy for a lower price. By the time the project is nearing completion most of the risk is gone which enables the purchaser to then resell the project to a more conservative buyer at a sharp increase in price.

In my visits to the Dominican Republic I have seem many situations where entire condo complexes were purchased by speculators looking to resell. Since the Dominican Republic has been a "hot" market for the last ten years very few of these speculators have lost money on their investments.

This new construction is not hard to find. Every real estate office is well aware of the new units being built and will usually show you a display model. In some cases only the blue prints are available. The companies building the units are usually foreign based and range from small investment partnerships to large development corporations.

When looking into new construction it is important to check the builder's track record. You need to make sure they have a habit of finishing what they started. You also want to make sure they finish their projects on schedule.

Pros

If you are planning on purchasing the new construction for the long term, by purchasing in the early phase you will most likely be paying less for the condo then if you were purchasing a similar unit second hand. This only goes for the early phase. If you purchase the same unit in a later phase of development you may wind up paying a premium.

You can be fairly certain that since it is new and you are purchasing from the builder there will not be any possible title problems that could occur if you purchased second hand.

If you are purchasing the condo as a speculator looking to resell you can put yourself in a position where you can turn a profit without laying out much initial capital. Most builders only require an initial deposit and then give you time to come up with the rest of the money. This buys you time to try to market the property for resell. If you are in the midst of a "hot" market it is possible to see appreciation on the value of the condo in a few short months. In this case you can sell the contract you possess for the property at an increase in price, leaving you with the spread.

Cons

This quick flip plan only works in the midst of a "hot" market. If the market turns there is a chance you may be stuck with the property. I only recommend putting the initial deposit down on a property if you are fully prepared to go through with the purchase if you find difficulty selling the project. In the United States right now we are going through a period where the market is flooded with new construction, and speculators are selling their contracts at a loss. I repeat; do not put a down payment on a property unless you are fully prepared to go through with the purchase.

Even with adequate research on a company there are no guarantees that this project will run as smooth as their previous projects. In the United States one of the biggest and well known development companies recently filed for bankruptcy. In a case like this all of the people who put down payments on the future construction are in limbo. While they will most likely eventually be returned their money, they will have to wait it out while the company gets its finances together.

There is less room for negotiation when purchasing new construction. If you are bargain hunting for a condo, there is a better chance in finding a motivated seller looking to unload their condo, then finding a builder willing to discount the price.

Investment potential for the novice
Purchasing new construction is a simple way to get your feet wet with Dominican Republic real estate. You have an opportunity to purchase a condo early in its development and ride the wave of appreciation to completion. This enables you the option of selling your contract for the condo before you even close on it. That is the easiest money you can make.

Of course this is all based on best case scenarios. Like I said earlier, you should only purchase a contract for new construction if you are fully prepared to go through with the sale.

Also, remember when looking into new construction it is important to research the track record of the company developing the projects. It is best to buy from a company with a solid track record.

Commercial Paper Investment

Since this book is about investing in the Dominican Republic I thought that I would include some other investment possibilities. Below John Schroder has given us another type of investment that requires less capital, management, and risk then purchasing real estate.

What is a commercial paper investment?

Many investors have asked about Commercial Paper in the Dominican Republic. Naturally they are interested in the high yields, but often ask, "What the heck is Commercial Paper"? For those investors that are unclear about certain investment terms, I am providing an explanation that should make things somewhat easier.

Bonds or Longer-Term Fixed Income Investments

For starters let's discuss what are known as "fixed income" investments. Fixed income normally refers to things like bonds, certificates of deposit or any type of investment whereby you are basically putting your money on deposit for a fixed period of time and for a fixed rate of interest. A bond is a type of fixed income investment and is in essence a loan. When you purchase a US government bond, you are loaning the government your money for a fixed time period and for a fixed rate of interest. When you purchase a corporate bond, from a company such as Pepsi or IBM, you are loaning that corporation your money in the same fashion. The term "Bond" is used when talking about a loan that is greater than one or two years. Most bonds are issued for five years, ten years, twenty-years and so on up to thirty years. When watching the financial news you will often hear the term US government "long bond". They are talking about 30 year US government bonds, which currently pay about 5.50% at the moment.

Interest on a bond investment is normally paid every six months to the investor. At the end of the bond time period or when it "matures", the principal amount is returned to the investor. As an example, if you invest $100,000 in a five-year bond at 6%, you will receive two interest checks every year, for a total of $6,000 every year that you own the bond (one check every six months for $3000). After five years, your $100,000 is returned to you. Interest on a bond is normally paid out every six months, but there are some bonds that pay interest monthly. It can be difficult to purchase long-term bonds in the Dominican Republic because many companies are fearful about borrowing money at a high rate for a long period of time. Just like investors who are looking for a mortgage, they do not want to be locked into a high interest loan if rates should go down in the future. Locking in a high rate over a long period of time is very good for the investor, but is not favorable for the entity borrowing the money.

Commercial paper or short term fixed income investments

Commercial paper is in effect a very short-term bond, usually for any period less than one year. When talking about commercial paper investments, we are in fact discussing a type of short-term investment for 30 days, 90 days, 180 days or any time frame that is one year or less. Most investors that understand a bank certificate of deposit can relate that to a commercial paper investment. The difference of course is that you are loaning your money directly to a company and not to the bank.

Most of the commercial paper issued in the Dominican Republic is for a minimum of 90 days. Investors that make this investment are in effect loaning their money to a company for a short-term need. Interest is usually paid monthly with a commercial paper investment and at the end of the 90 days, the principal or initial investment is returned to the investor. When we work with our clients that are interested in the higher yields found in Dominican Peso Investments, we have made special arrangements with the brokers we work with so your monthly interest is automatically credited to your Dominican Peso Bank Savings Account. This way this is no hassle cashing your monthly interest check and you always have access to your money via your ATM card (which can be used worldwide at any bank machine that is a member of PLUS or CIRRUS). The commercial paper can also be registered in your name directly or if you prefer, in the name of your corporation, foundation or trust.

Why are the rates higher in the Dominican?

Money is a commodity, like oil, silver, bananas or coffee. When it is in short supply, the price goes up. The price of money is interest rates and when it is in short supply, interest rates are higher. This is the situation in the Dominican Republic and elsewhere. Many companies either need money for a short term need or they do not want to issue longer term bonds and would prefer to continuously re-borrow every 90 days at the prevailing rate. The thinking behind this is that the company will not become locked into a very high rate on a long-term basis if the interest rates come down. Part of this business philosophy has come about because rates in the Dominican Republic have in fact come down from a high of over 30% a few years back.

Some companies do have a need for US dollars in order to trade with the United States. Since there are often not enough dollars in the banking system, companies must attract individual investors by offering a better rate of return than can be found elsewhere. An example of this can be seen with Reid & company, a 50 year-old Dominican conglomerate that happens to have a vehicle and heavy-duty equipment distributorship. They recently offered up to a 14%

interest rate for 90-day commercial paper in US dollars so they could re-stock their inventory. Since the car manufacturers in Detroit want to be paid in dollars, not pesos, they needed to borrow US dollars for this purpose. Investors therefore had an opportunity to take advantage and get a good rate of return from a large and well managed local company.

The interest rates of course will change weekly, depending upon the market and demand.

For more information on Commercial Paper Investment contact:

Ascot Advisory
BM-1134
8357 West Flagler Street – Suite D
Miami, Florida 33144-2072
Telephone (809) 334-5387 or (809) 293-9427

Chapter 4

How economic cycles affect real estate

Although this book is mainly about purchasing real estate in the Dominican Republic I wanted to go over some basic real estate concepts. Let's call this part of the book Real Estate Economics 101.

The vacation/resort area real estate in the Dominican Republic is affected just as much by the world economy as it the local Dominican economy. That is why it is important to know how this will affect your real estate purchase. It may also influence your decision on when to buy, or when to sell.

Economic cycles have always been with us. Since the dawn of time there have been periods of feast, and periods of famine. The ancient civilizations knew that during times of feast you always had to prepare for times of famine.

In today's world, we track economic cycles by the relative strength or weakness of money, our medium of exchange. There are prolonged periods of boom. In these times businesses are flourishing, real estate is appreciating, workers are in high demand, jobs are abundant, and money is readily exchanging hands. More money is being spent on goods and services and more money is being lent for real estate and business investments. During this period, usually 4-8 years, people tend to think the good times will last forever.

The amount of investors and speculators making purchases creates a demand that fuels price increases. Every Joe Shmoe thinks they are a savvy investor who can buy low and sell high later on. During these times investments are based more on riding a wave of emotion than on the fundamentals. When it starts to become clear that the expectations these investors had for their investments will not be met, price start dropping. Skeptical, unconfident investors panic and start "dumping." Prices plummet even further. The economy slowly heads in the opposite direction.

Here are some common reasons that fuel a recession:

Workers demanding increased wages due to a shortage of available help

Material shortages

External factors; such as how the War in Iraq is driving the price of oil up

War

Acts of congress that affects the economy such as tax increases

Actions of the Federal Reserve that make money tighter and more expensive. The Federal Reserve controls both money supply and interest rates. The fed uses its control to curb inflation in good times and to supply money to the economy in bad times.

We have most recently experienced a recession in the United States in the early two thousands. This recession was fueled by the stock market not reaching the high expectations placed on it by many no so knowledgeable investors. Once the market began going soft, the masses panicked and started unloading their investments at a loss. This caused prices to plummet even further. Stocks that had been previously trading at $50-$60 could now be bought for $2 or $3. During this time people became hesitant to re-enter the market keeping prices stagnant for a few years. The only thing keeping the market in the United States from completing tanking over the last few years was the sharp demand in the housing market. Now that the prices of stocks have begun to increase again the general public feels confident to come back into the stock market. This is how the recovery begins.

A smart and careful long term investor knows that throughout history each subsequent boom has reached a higher level than the previous boom. A smart investor maintains a long term perspective. They avoid getting caught up in speculative fever in good times, and act more conservatively. A smart investor views bad times as providing investment opportunities for the long run.

By having and sticking to a long term plan, as well as being knowledgeable about the market you are entering, you can avoid getting rushed in temporary bust periods. If you follow the plan of your investment through good and bad weather you will see them continually grow in value.

It is also never easy to tell when we are at the top or bottom of a market. If you carefully research your investments and thoroughly evaluate the intrinsic value, you should be able to avoid overpaying during booms- and like-wise getting scared and selling prematurely in busts.

Economic Cycles and Real Estate

How does this all relate to your desire to purchase real estate in a far off Caribbean island? Well, as with stock prices the general public tends to follow the trends like sheep. If the prices of real estate are going up, they start speculating in real estate, helping to fuel further price increases. This has been seen in the United States over the last ten years where real estate prices have reached all time highs.

In the United States during this period everyone wanted to become a real estate investor. This drove up prices of single family homes, multi family, commercial, and vacation homes. Any real estate agent in the Dominican Republic will tell you that when the United States is in a period of boom, the Dominican Republic real estate market is booming. And when there is a ripple in the United States market, a wave crashed down on the Dominican Republic.

So, assuming that you've purchased a property in the Dominican Republic, how should you respond during a time of economic boom? Your choices are to either a) Do nothing or b) sell the property. Let's examine each of these options.

- *Do nothing.* If you've purchased a well located property that makes decent rental income or is paying off its mortgage, the best advice might be to stay put. In the long term the value of your property should continue to rise.
- *Sell the property.* If you own several properties, you might sell one or two of them to use the cash to pay off the mortgages on the properties

you keep. Or you might choose to save the money from the sale to use as available cash to take advantages of possible future slumps.

As you can see, property prices are also affected by changes in economic and speculative conditions. In periods of boom, the goal is to save, not only to protect you from economic downturns, but-just as important- to be able to take advantage of them instead of being one of them financially hurt by them.

For example when the economy is on a downward trend, real estate properties may be:

*Available at distressed prices from panicked holders
*Abandoned by speculators
*Temporarily vacant as a result of the economic slowdown, and selling low.
* Foreclosed by lenders anxious to dispose of them, even at a loss.

Speculation

Over the last couple chapters I've talked about speculation quite a bit. If you are going to be a real estate investor you must understand the role speculation plays in the economy in general, and real estate in particular. Speculator's actions influence prices in all areas of the economy. When there is an increase in speculative buying, prices go up due to high demand. But when the speculators start selling, prices drop equally fast.

It can be said that the increasing interest in the Dominican Republic is based on speculation. I tend to disagree. I believe that ten years ago it was speculative interest. No one really knew whether or not the country would take off as a leading Caribbean tourist destination. Because of this, the people who purchased real estate in the Dominican Republic ten years ago have made quite a return on investment.

The people investing in the Dominican Republic now are fewer speculators than bargain hunters. The speculators proved years ago that the DR had tremendous potential. It is only now that the investment potential has been brought to the attention of the general public.

Of course there will always be speculating. What will be the next hot area? As places like Punta Cana, Sosua, and Samana have seen explosive growth, investors are frantically looking for the next "it" location.

Chapter 5

Calculating Long and Short Term Profit Potential

Over the past 10 years in the United States we've witnessed one of the greatest boom periods in American real estate we have seen in some time. It seemed that any which way you invested you were bound to make a dollar at the end of the day. Novice investors were buying property with nothing down and then turning around and selling the same property months later at a significant profit.

In a boom cycle it is possible for this to occur. In a down cycle this is a recipe for disaster. There are basic fundamentals to investing in real estate that should be applied to your potential purchase in the Dominican Republic, or for that matter, anywhere you choose to invest. From a strictly investment standpoint, two good guidelines are (1) to buy property in a good area that has been overbuilt, and (2) to buy in deteriorated, but well located, areas on the brink of rehabilitation.

In applying this principles to the Dominican Republic we would not so much consider deteriorated areas so much as areas that have yet to have outside money invested to build it up. If you keep up with the news about the island you will constantly read stories of big investors such as Donald Trump, pouring millions into certain areas of the Dominican. A speculator's success lies in predicting which area will be the next to receive this kind of funding, and purchase land before the big money comes in and drives prices way up.

Although there is big money to be made in speculation, there is big risk, and I would not suggest on using this formula for your first investment property in the Dominican. Why? Because unless you have some people in high places living down there, chances are you won't be aware of these areas until it is too late. Any area that you "speculate" on will be more of a guess.

Instead for your first investment I would suggest purchasing in a prime area that has been overbuilt and is experiencing a temporary decline in price. In a later chapter I will discuss how to locate and evaluate these properties.

The rest of this chapter will take a number crunching view of the potential of real estate investments.

Real Estate Profit Sources

1.) *Positive Cash Flow*. A well located property in a good area has the potential to generate rental income even after operating expenses and loan payments.
2.) *Appreciation*. Properties in certain areas of the Dominican Republic have more than tripled in value in the last 8 years.
3.) *Leverage*. Properties appreciate while the debt stays constant. Leverage is the use of debt to increase buying power of your cash down payment.

I will include examples in this chapter that will expand on each of these profit sources. To make this simple and easy to understand I am going to use the same purchase criteria for the three profit source examples. We are going to pretend that you've purchased a condo in Samana for $200,000 with a down payment of $50,000. The mortgage is $150,000 at 8 percent interest only; there is no amortization (or payoff) of the mortgage. At time of purchase rental income of the property was $20,000 a year.

These examples are simply to show where the money is made from a real estate transaction. In a later chapter I will go into more details about what the numbers actually mean, and how to go about finding properties that will get the best return on investment. I will also go into more detail about the types of financing available for purchasing real estate in the Dominican Republic.

Positive Cash Flow

The first calculation that we'll make is to determine cash flow return on the $50,000 down payment investment:

Profit before debt service $20,000
Interest on $150,000 at 8% $12,000
Net cash flow after debt service $8,000

$8,000 cash flow divided by the $50,000 down payment = 16% cash return on investment.

Not a bad return on investment. Not bad at all. But there we are using an interest only mortgage. Let's look at the same example and calculate the effect of a self liquidating mortgage. A self liquidating mortgage is one that has a level of payments over a certain number of years, which includes interest and principle. The payments are structured so that at the end of the mortgage, the principle portion of the monthly payments has paid off the mortgage.

Profit before debt service $20,000
Debt service on $150,000 at 8% $16,500
Net Cash flow $3,500

$3,500 cash flow divided by the $50,000 down payment = 7% cash flow

To the cash flow of $3,500, we must add the mortgage payment, or $4,500; your return then is:

Cash flow $3,500
Amortization of loan $4,500
Total $8,000

The total return of $8,000 divided by the initial cash investment of $50k = 16%

Appreciation

What's missing from the previous examples? The second source of real estate profit, the appreciation. In the previous chapters I mentioned that the long term increase in value of real estate results from its irreplaceability, general economic improvements, and inflation, among other factors. For example assume you have bought a property for cash, that you have held it for ten years, and that it has doubled in value.

Initially
Original purchase price $200,000
Original cash flow $20,000 a year

10 years later
Value $400,000
Cash flow $40,000 a year

The profit is twofold: from appreciation and cash flow income, that is, increase and value.

Appreciation (increase in value)
Future value $400,000
Less original price   ($200,000)
Net appreciation $200,000

Income

Original annual income $20,000
Final annual income $40,000

Income goes up and the value of the property rises, and property value rise as the income goes up. You will find, as I explain in a later chapter, that with vacation homes the increase in rental income does not usually rise as fast as the property appreciates. But for the sake of this lesson I will pretend it does.

Average income over the 10-year period is the original income, plus final income, divided by 2. In this case, average income per year computes as follows: Initial income of $20,000, plus income 10 years later of $40,000, equals an average of $30,000 per year. Over the 10 year period, the total income was the $30,000 average times ten years, or:

$30,000 X 10 years= $300,000

At the end of 10 years you will have:

Property worth $400,000
Accumulated income $300,000
Total return $700,000
Or 3.5 times your original investment of $200,000

Remember, this example assumes an all cash purchase; furthermore, it ignores the additional interest earned by the annual cash flow of $20,000 to $40,000 per year. If we take into account the interest or other returns generated by the annual cash flow, the profit will be even higher.

Leverage

Our second example of appreciation will include the third source of profit from real estate transactions: effects of leverage or borrowed funds. We'll again use the $200,000 Samana condo with $150,000 loan at 8%, and for simplification we'll ignore the effects of amortization of the loan.

Now let's look at our example. Here to you've held the property for 10 years:

Price of property (initially) $200,000
Mortgage $150,000
Down payment $50,000

Original cash flow $20,000 per year
Future cash flow $40,000 per year
Average cash flow $30,000 per year

Less interest on $150,000 at 8%   ($12,000)
Average cash flow after interest   ($18,000)

After 10 years

Value of property $400,000
Mortgage (assuming no pay down of principle) $150,000
Net Equity $250,000

Plus 10-year cash flow

Average annual income	$30,000
Less annual interest	($12,000)
Net annual cash flow	$18,000

Cash flow over 10 years	$180,000
Total after 10 years	$430,000
Original cash investment	$ 50,000

Our original cash investment of $50,000 increased to $430,000 in just 10 years. This is an example of a well located condo in a booming area. The numbers show how much potential there is.

Let's review: Assuming 7.5% per year appreciation of a property, on an all-cash purchase with 10 percent annual cash flow, your initial investment would typically increase 3.5 times over the 10 years. This includes cash income and appreciation.

In fact, assuming reasonable leverage (or borrowed money) in the same scenario, usually your investment would increase 8.5 times! That is the effect of leverage- using other people's money to grow your own. You pay the lender a fixed amount, plus the lenders money back, and the rest is yours. Both cases- all cash purchase and a purchase using debt- demonstrates the profitability of real estate over the long term.

These are simple examples solely to show you how the money is made. While you can say that these numbers seem inflated, in some cases they may be considered conservative. It's all about choosing the right property, in the right place, at the right time. In the next chapter I will help to learn how to go about doing just that.

Chapter 6

Finding and Evaluating Properties for Purchase

Who would have thought just 10 years ago how easy it would become to search for real estate oversees. I am lucky enough to have begun my international real estate career after the rise of the internet. I could not imagine how difficult it would have been before the invention of the internet to go about purchasing property in another country.

The process would have involved hours of long distance phone calls, mailing brochures of properties, countless trips to the desired location, and a lot of faith in a lot of people whose faces you've never seen.

Lucky for you, that is no longer the case. Yes, the beauty of technology allows us to do virtually all of our shopping (real estate included) from the comfort of our own home. Technology allows us to communicate with people in another country with a few clicks of the keyboard, for next to pennies. It allows to research for endless hours without a trip to the library. It gives us the freedom of choice, to see as many properties as possible, and to talk to as many knowledgeable sources as possible.

Yes, you could not have picked a better time to begin your search for real estate in the Dominican Republic.

Finding Properties

Just like in your home country there are numerous sources for finding real estate properties. In this chapter I will go over the most common places to look for real estate. In the appendix at the end of this book I will give a detailed list of specific websites, and companies that I have had luck with in the past.

Here is quick rundown of the ways to find to properties in the Dominican.

- Real Estate brokers (in person and online)
- Dominican Republic Real estate specialists
- Word of mouth
- Advertisements online and in printed periodicals
- Mailing lists

Real Estate Brokers

More than likely no matter what source you use to begin your search for a suitable property in the Dominican Republic, at some point you will need the help of a real estate broker. I do not recommend purchasing your first property in the Dominican Republic without the help of a real estate professional.

It is a broker's job to bring together buyers and sellers. If it doesn't get done, they don't get paid. So you can bet that they will be doing everything they possibly can to find you the right property. (This is not to say that there are not unscrupulous agents out there. There are, and I will help you look out for and stay clear of them.)

A major benefit of the use of a broker in locating properties is that they are the most knowledgeable about the inventory at hand. A good broker knows his/her market and knows exactly what you should be able to purchase at a particular price. A good broker also knows other important information such as: neighborhood status, local trends, and places to invest for maximum returns, what areas are declining, and more. A competent broker should be able to answer all of your questions. A broker will also be able to introduce you to the other real estate professionals you will need in your rolodex. These people include attorneys, title agencies, appraisers, insurance brokers, builders, architects, engineers, lenders, and management companies.

The Dominican Republic real estate system is different than it is here in the United States. For one thing, there is no MLS. This means that there is not one central hub where all the houses on the market are listed. There are also very few exclusive listings. This means that basically any broker can sell any house. Basically how it works in the Dominican Republic is that when someone decides to sell their house/condo/hotel they go to as many agencies as they can to get the word out. These agencies now list the properties on their personal websites. Once they've listed the property for sale, other agencies usually pay attention to their competition, and when they see a new house listed they will then go about trying to sell that house as well.

My first reaction was to think that it was much more complicated down there. But in hindsight I would say that it is actually a lot simpler. One of the draw backs to their system is that basically anyone can present themselves as a realtor. This is because without the laws we have here; they can earn a commission if they sell a house without taking a test, working under a broker, or being registered with the state. This means that you have to be particular careful selecting a broker.

There are a couple reasons that make finding a good real estate broker in the Dominican Republic a difficult task.

1) There are a lot less laws about who can act as a real estate professional so you have to be careful of fly-by- nighters. Fly-by-nighters are those people who've just recently entered the profession on a whim. They haven't had any real training in real estate and will probably not be practicing real estate by the time you meet them again. I've met many of these people during my trips to the Dominican. Most Dominicans are aware that the property on the island is becoming more and more attractive to foreigners. Sensing that they can make a quick buck they introduce themselves as a real estate professional to unsuspecting foreigners. While not all of them are crooks looking to scam you out of money, they are certainly not the most qualified to be helping you along in the purchase process.

2) Lack of time is the other reason that makes it so difficult to find a good broker in the Dominican Republic. Being that you will most likely have limited time to look at properties while in the Dominican Republic, often you decide to go with the first broker willing to drive you around. This is not a smart choice.

The fact that you do have only limited time, you want to ensure that you are spending it with the most qualified agent out there. The good agents are usually busy, so you want to schedule your time with them in advance.

I am not going to scare you with horror stories from people who have not had the most pleasant experiences with the realtors that they've chosen. Instead my goal is to help you choose a broker that is qualified to handle as important a process as buying a piece of real estate in a foreign country.

Finding a qualified broker

As with the hiring of anybody in the service industry the best way to find a broker is through the positive recommendation of someone you trust. In the United States this is how a good broker earns his high paydays. He/she does such a great job for his clients that they almost feel obligated to refer him/her to their friends. This is a great way to start your search. Ask around your social circle, any local real estate investment clubs, your neighborhood realtor, and see if any of them know of a good agent working down there. You will be surprised at how many people may have information like this. My philosophy is, "everyone knows someone who knows someone." At the very least this is a great way to start. It may turn out that the person that they know may not work the area that you are interested in, but maybe they can recommend a realtor that is qualified for your area.

There are some drawbacks to using this approach. First, unless your social circle contains many real estate savvy people, you may find it hard to get any good leads. Sometimes people are overeager to try to help that they may refer you to someone that they don't have personal knowledge of their experience or qualifications. I have acquaintances that will take someone's business card and then refer this person out without ever having worked with the person. People like to feel like they've made a contribution, but while their intention is good, sometimes the consequences are unwanted. Whenever someone refers you someone ask them if they've ever worked with this person before. If they haven't ask them if anyone they know has. If they say yes, ask them if it is possible to get in contact with the person who has worked with them. This will give you the chance to get first hand answers to any questions you have about the broker in question.

Another way to find a broker is to make use of modern technology. There is an abundance of Dominican Republic real estate brokers listed on the internet. If you are planning a trip down to the Dominican Republic I suggest contacting several of them via internet. Most of the websites list the broker's email address. Use this as an opportunity to interview them to see who might be your most compatible. Also remember that there is no rule that says you can't meet with several agents when you get down there. I do not recommend working with too many different brokers. You may wind up spreading yourself too thin. My motto has always been you will have better luck finding your ideal property working with one or two high quality brokers then working with twenty fly by nighters.

When you interview these brokers I suggest asking some of these questions:

- Will there be any language barrier? If you are not fluent in Spanish you want to make sure that the person assisting you will be fluent in your native language. Real estate jargon is complicated enough; there is no need to make it more difficult by embracing a language barrier.
- How long have they been working in their particular area. You want an agent who has good knowledge of the location. If the agent has just moved to Punta Cana from Santiago, chances are they're not your best selection to spend your limited time with. Ideally you want someone who has been working in a local real estate market for at least 1 year.
- Ask them what price range they feel most comfortable selling. I've met quite a few brokers who will not bother to show properties that sell for less than $100,000. I've met other brokers who have said 90% of their business is condos under $50,000.
- Ask them what they specialize in. Most independent brokers specialize in one of the following categories: Homes- single family dwellings, including condos. Commercial, including multifamily residential, retail, offices, and net leases. Industrial, including warehouses and public storage. Land, including farm acreage. It is important that you find a broker who specializes in the type of real estate that you plan on purchasing.
- Ask them if they have any references that you can check. If they are as qualified as they say they are they should have no problem providing you with names, phone numbers, and email addresses of satisfied clients.

Once they give you the phone number or email, contact the person and ask them about their experience with the broker. This will also give you an opportunity to learn a little bit more about the whole process of buying in the Dominican Republic.

Another way to find a broker is to go to a large firm in your home country such as Century 21, Caldwell Banker, or Remax. These firms all have branches in the Dominican Republic. They will be happy to refer you to one of their sister branches down there. This tactic is good because you get a little security of working with a global firm. The drawback to this is that they may not refer you to the most qualified agent down there.

What you don't want to do is arrive in the Dominican Republic without having previously arranged to view property with a broker. Not only will you waste time having to drive to all the local agencies interviewing agents, but when you do find an agent you will have to start the process from the very beginning. If you had already been dealing with an agent they will have your agenda set up for you before you arrive. This allows you to make the best use of your limited time on the island. Also, because you will be in a hurry to go out and view property you run a better risk of having a lapse in judgment in choosing your broker. There is nothing worse than realizing four days into a five day trip that you're dealing with an incompetent broker.

When you meet your broker you should expect them to interview you and go over your requirements and desires. They should also go over your financial capabilities with you, as well as your motive for buying, and desired financial rate of return. Here is a list of what else you can expect from a good broker:

- Examine lists of properties for sale that are appropriate for the buyer,
- Contact other brokers for additional appropriate properties for sale.
- Arrange property inspections.
- Help buyer through the negotiation process.
- Introduce the buyer to mortgage brokers to help him or her get financing.
- Facilitate the transaction to ensure it goes as smooth as possible.

These are just some of the things you can expect from a good broker. At any time you don't feel like your broker is serving you to the best of their ability do not hesitate to find an alternate broker. Don't worry about hurting their feelings, or denying them a commission. This is too big a step to trust with an amateur or nonprofessional.

Dominican Republic Real Estate Specialists

Another good way to find properties in the Dominican Republic is to get in contact with a Dominican Republic Real Estate Specialist. This is what my former company Mydrlife.com is.

What a company like this does is they act as a "buyer's agent." They usually are located in your home country. It can be an intimidating process trying to contact oversees brokers, not really understanding the process of buying down in the Dominican, and not having any clue who to turn to for legal advice, financial advice, or rental/management advice. This is where a company like Mydrlife.com comes in. What you can expect from a company like this:

- They have listings of the entire inventory (property for sale in the Dominican) and have contact with all of the brokers down there. They know which brokers specialize in what types of properties, and will match you with the most appropriate broker for your needs.
- Go over lists of properties for sale and appropriate for the buyer
- Contact brokers in the Dominican Republic for additional properties.
- Help you set up an itinerary for your trip to the Dominican.
- They are aware of your financing options for your particular country.
- They will help you with management and rental duties of the property.
- They will be on top of the transaction from start to finish helping you relax a little bit more.

You can find companies like this all over the internet. I highly suggest choosing a company located in your home country. If possible try to find a company located as close to your home as possible. This will enable you to meet your representative personally. It will also help them better introduce your financing options, because they differ from state to state.

Word of Mouth

Although in the general practice of purchasing real estate investments word of mouth is usually a valuable means in finding a good property, assuming you're talking to the right people, it is a little less fruitful when dealing with properties in the Dominican Republic.

This is not say that you shouldn't keep your ears open as sometimes the best leads come from the most unexpected sources. It is my belief, that when you're looking to purchase a property somewhere, you should let as many people know your intention as possible. You never know who might step up to the plate with a great lead.

There are certain people that tend to know people looking to sell properties overseas more often. Here is a list of people you may want to pay special attention to. These are professionals that deal with people who might be selling a property.

- Accountants
- Local real estate agents
- Divorce attorneys
- Members at your local real estate clubs
- Travel agents

If you're down in the Dominican it is also possible to find property through word of mouth. I don't usually recommend this since it is easy to be taken advantage of down there if they sense that you're inexperienced with the island.

Most of the locals won't be good sources of information regarding properties for sale. A better source of information might be the other foreign property owners living down there. Many of the expats become friendly down there, and often they'll mention to one another if they are looking to sell. If you mingle with the foreign owners enough they may be able to introduce you to someone looking to sell. I'm sure that you'll find owners who would love to leave the broker out of it, as they will avoid a hefty commission. But for your first purchase down there I really don't recommend purchasing without the help and assistance of a good broker. Remember the saying, "A good broker is worth his weight in gold."

Advertisements Online and in Printed Periodicals

In this day and age all one has to do is type "Dominican Republic real estate" into a search engine and you will find hundreds of properties for sale. In the appendix of this book I list several of the best sites for farming for properties.

The whole idea of advertising online is part of the reason that purchasing a vacation home oversees has become such a great form of investment. In this day and age almost everyone is online. We use it for everything from purchasing books, paying bills, price comparing MP3 players, grocery shopping, booking vacations, all the way to watching movies and downloading our favorite new songs. With the amount of people logged into the internet increasing everyday it is safe to say that this marketplace is absolutely tremendous.

It is a great advantage for someone looking to sell their vacation home. Whereas before they would maybe list it in a local newspaper, now they can put it on a website that can be potentially viewed by a hundred million people. Do you think this increases the chance of a sale? You bet it does!

The whole advent of the internet has taken something far off and remote like buying a home on an island in the Caribbean and made it seem as simple as a few clicks of the keyboard. Sure there is more to it than that. But man have we come along way!

Realistically you can go online and view hundreds of properties in a matter of minutes. Most websites have features that allow the seller to create a virtual tour of the property. This is basically a camera that walks you through the property letting you zoom in on things you want to see clearer.

There are also many newspapers, magazines, and journals that have online counterparts; and especially in the case of newspapers, its easy to access their classified sections, and from there to find the real estate listings. Most of the listings in the classifieds won't give you the benefit of pictures, but they will list the broker's number who can then email you all the information you want on the property.

There are several benefits of browsing through listings online before meeting with a real estate broker.

- You get to see a large variety of what's available
- You get a feel for what you will pay for certain types of property
- In most cases you get the contact number of the owner or broker selling the property.
- You can suggest properties to the broker that you are interested in, thus saving time once you arrive in the Dominican Republic.

The major drawback of viewing properties online

Here is a quick story to summarize why viewing properties online can sometimes be misleading if you aren't also working with a qualified broker from your particular area of interest.

William, a friend of mine, was looking to purchase a condo in the Cabarete area. He had previously been to the Dominican, so he was somewhat familiar with the area. He was in contact with several brokers down there but wasn't working with any of them exclusively. Most of his property hunting was done by browsing various websites for listings in his price range.

One weekend he came across a listing on the website Craigslist.com. The property was listed for $80,000. The ad described it as beachfront, in the heart of Cabarete. He quickly dialed the owner's phone number. The owner turned out to be from the same state in the United States as him. They discussed the property for a bit, and then the owner emailed him a few more pictures.

In the course of the conversation the owner mentioned that there were several other people interested in the condo. William felt this was an opportunity of a lifetime. All the brokers he had talked to told him that he couldn't touch beachfront condos in Cabarete for under $150,000. He chalked his "deal" up to the fact that the owner wasn't being represented by a broker. Not wanting to miss this opportunity he quickly booked a trip down to the Dominican Republic to view the property in person.

Because he felt he was getting such a great deal he didn't want to jeopardize it by asking one of the brokers he was working with about the particular property. The last thing he wanted was for a broker to call the owner and tell him he could get a higher price if they listed it with them.

The moment that he arrived at the property he realized his mistake. The property was located right outside Cabarate in a seedier part of town. The condo was by no means beach front. The condo was old and in need of quite a bit of work inside.

At this point he called the broker he had been talking to and mentioned the condo and asked his opinion on the price. The broker told him that the price is right in line with what it should be. And if he was interested in less than desirable locations he could show him a dozen in the same price range.

The moral of the story is you can't fall in love with a property over the internet. If you find a property you think you might be interested it, run the property by a broker who knows that market. They will tell you everything you need to know about the property. They will know if the price is in line. They will know how the area is. They will know how "rentable" the property is.

On that trip down there my friend wound up buying a brand new condo on the beach in Cabarete, but he paid $180,000 for it.

Printed Periodicals

If you are searching for listings in the Dominican Republic another place that you can look for properties is newspapers and magazines. Brokers will usually advertise in these classifieds to cater to the folks who still aren't internet savvy. These advertisements will usually give a little information about the property and include the broker's phone number or email address.

You probably won't find too many Dominican Republic listings in the local papers, but the newspapers with wider circulations, such as *The New York Post,*

The Wall Street Journal, and *The Washington Post*, contain ads from all over the world.

You can also find properties for sale in certain magazines. Most of the magazines that will list properties for sale oversees will be catered to the higher end market. Unless you are looking for a custom designed villa, or a huge plot of beachfront land, this is probably not an avenue that will produce many good leads.

Newsletters

Another good way to find potential properties for sale is sign up for as many real estate investment newsletters as possible. Most of these are free to get on the list. They make their money by charging people to advertise.

Since the main people running ads in these newsletters are other real estate investors there is always the chance that you will run across someone trying to cash out of their investment.

This is not a sure fire way to find the largest selection of properties but the newsletters often contain other valuable insights about real estate investing in general. My philosophy has always been to immerse myself in any subject that I've decided to pursue. These newsletters are a great way to stay a head in the game. The latest news and happenings in the real estate and real estate financing world are discussed. The good newsletters tend to be ahead of the trends. So don't be surprised if these newsletters often mention investing in the Dominican Republic.

Evaluating Properties for Investment Potential

Now that you realize that it is not that difficult to find properties for sale in the Dominican Republic, you can begin to search them out, look at some, and evaluate them as potential investments. While some of you may be purchasing more with your heart then your head (and that's fine if you're looking for something to retire in) the rest of you need a good formula and guide for evaluating properties.

Although the steps will vary depending on exactly what kind of property you decide to purchase, these are some basic guidelines:

1. First you must gather all the available information on the property-the seller should provide you or your broker with a description of the property, floor sizes, number of rooms, income and expenses, and any other information you request.
2. You should examine the property and take a ride around the neighborhood.
3. You should try to estimate what your monthly expenses will be, and figure out how often you can realistically have the place rented out.
4. Figure out what kind of return you would like to make and see if this property fits your guidelines.
5. Compare this property will similar properties for sale. This will give you an idea if the price is in range. It will also give you an idea where to start your offer if you decide to make a bid for the property.

As a side note, I always recommend flying down to the Dominican Republic and viewing the property yourself before you make any offers. The story I told earlier about my friend William only emphasizes this point.

For those of you who are deciding whether or not to purchase a pre existing villa or buy land and build a new one, I have included a small list of some of things you will need to build your own.

- You will need preliminary zoning approvals
- You will need to work with architects, engineers, contractors, plumbers…
- You will need to get construction loans (Financing construction projects overseas is not an easy task, especially if you have no previous experience)
- You need to be able to handle cost overruns caused by delays and other construction related problems
- You need to wait for completion for even the possibility of any rental income to offset expenses.
- You will have to purchase all of the furnishings

While I'm not trying to totally dissuade you from building your own villa, condo, hotel, or the like, I am trying to make you aware that it is not by any means a simple process.

A Formula for analyzing investment properties

The first step in analyzing a potential Dominican Republic investment property is to figure out all of the possible expenses for the year. This includes all of the possible bills associated with this property. These expenses include things like: loan repayment, taxes, insurance, management fees, service fees for cable and internet, electric and water bills, cleaning, landscaping.

If you are purchasing a property from a seller who has owned the property for several years they should be able to give you a pretty detailed summary of what these cost will entail. But you have to remember that you can not ever go fully on the seller's word. There are always expenses that they tend to leave out or "forget." But after viewing all of their expenses you should have a pretty good idea.

Once you know what all of your expenses will be for the year for the property you need to figure out your breakeven point. Your breakeven point is the point where your income for the property meets the expenses projected for the entire year. This is how you know whether you will be making a profit or a loss. Remember, when you're purchasing a real estate investment such as this, your goal is first and foremost to own the property with little or nothing coming out of your pocket after the initial down payment. This gives you a nice vacation home that is appreciating, and allows you a nice tax shelter.

Everyone has different goals when it comes to their particular investment. The real estate professionals you talk to down there should be able to educate you on the potential for each of these properties to meet your particular goals. You need to remember though, that these people are not the ones buying the property, you are. This means that ultimately you have to have a personal formula that you use when evaluating each and every property.

I have a formula that I use that I learned from author, Christine Karpinski, in her book "How to Rent Vacation Properties by Owner." Her formula is a simple formula that really can be applied to any type of property that you intend on renting out. Here is her formula:

If your monthly mortgage payment is less than or equal to one peak week rental, and you rent approximately 17 weeks per year, you will break even.

- Your mortgage payments (including taxes and insurance) should be roughly equal to, or less than, one peak week's earnings.
- Peak weeks-the highest earning weeks of the rental season. Usually there are 12 peak weeks in a rental year. So if you rent these 12 weeks, you will have enough revenue to pay your mortgage payments for the entire year.
- Other costs, including bills for your phone, power, cable, dues, are paid by your earning from approximately five off-week rentals. So, even by renting only 17 weeks out of the year, you can still break even. These other costs as you can see are paid for.

One of the beautiful things about the Dominican Republic is, unlike vacation homes in most places, it is not that difficult to find a property that will fit into this formula. Although the prices of property in the Dominican have steadily risen over the past 10 years, so has the influx of tourists. This means that the rental rates have increased along with the price of property. If you look at markets such as the United States or even other islands in the Caribbean you will find that the price increases of the properties are often much more significant than the rental increases.

Here is an example of using this formula to evaluate the potential of a condo for sale in the Dominican Republic.

The facts about the property:

The asking price of the condo is $150,000
You have $45,000 to put down
The loan is 70% of the value or $105,000
Your monthly loan payment with taxes and insurance is $1050
Various expenses for the year come to $9,000
Peak week rental for this property is $1,400

Off week rentals are from $800-1000

Looking at this example, the property would need to bring in $21,600 to break even. This means you would only need to rent the property for 16 weeks at $1,400. This property definitely fits into the formula but there are still other questions that you have to ask yourself.

How often can you get this condo rented?

When I visit the Dominican Republic I try to talk to as many property owners as I can to see how often their property is being rented. This gives me an idea of the rental demand for certain areas. Another way I scout out rental demand is I go to websites like VRBO.com and view the various properties listed on there. All of the listings have a little calendar letting you know when the property is available, and when it is booked. This is a good way to get a feel for how often these properties are being rented.

I also judge based on my experience finding an adequate place to rent. When I first began visiting the Dominican a few years back it was relatively easy to find an available condo or villa in my price range for the week I desired. Over the years though, it has become more and more difficult. It seems I have to book further in advance to get the property I desire. This is particularly true of the peak weeks. Another way to determine how often a condo will rent is to ask the current owner to see his income/expense sheet. This is only possible if the current owner had been renting it. If so, it is a great way to get a feel for how often this property can rent. If the vacancy rate is a little higher than you like, you don't necessarily have to be discouraged, in a later chapter I will show you ways to increase the amount of weeks the property will rent.

Rental Rates

Another fact that you need to consider is the rental rates. The rental rates in the Dominican Republic have stayed pretty consistent with the appreciation the country has seen. This is mainly due to the increase in tourism the country has seen over the past 12 years. When you are looking at rental rates an important thing to consider is how this area will hold up against time. Is it an area that will continue to attract tourists, allowing the rental rates to increase with inflation, or is it an area that is slowly eroding, and losing its tourist to an up and coming neighbor? You have to remember that you are not the one who determines what the rental rates are. If everyone in town drops their rates you will have to lower your to compete with the market.

The variable of other costs

For this property I figured in $9,000 a year in other expenses besides the mortgage payment and insurance. The other costs for this condo include things like cable/internet, condo dues, electric, water, and gas bill, phone lines, maid services, etc. These numbers will probably wind up a little lower than $9,000 a year. You have to be aware that these numbers can fluctuate. You also have to take into consideration that you might be hiring a management company to rent this condo for you. If you take into consideration the fact that these companies can take anywhere from 10%-30% of the weekly rent, this could significantly affect your bottom line. Let's say for argument sake that you had a management company that rented the condo 12 of the 16 weeks that it was rented. Let's say that their fee was 20% of the weekly rent. This means that $3,360 a year would be going to them. That number could increase if they were to find the renter more than 12 times. This means that you would need to rent the property 3 more times to break even.

As you can see there are several factors that can influence your decision as to whether or not the property fits into your formula. Below I'm going to use an example of a property that doesn't fit into the formula.

The asking price of the condo is $150,000
You have $45,000 to put down
The loan is 70% of the value or $105,000
Your monthly loan payment with taxes and insurance is $1050
Various expenses for the year come to $12,000
Peak week rental for this property is $800
Off week rentals are from $600-650

Looking at this property it would need $24,600 a year to break even. This means you would need to rent the property 31 times to break even. This property doesn't fit into the formula. Does this mean that the property is definitely not a good investment? No. If you consider the three factors; number of week's rented, rental rates, and variable expenses you may see that property still has potential. Maybe the property is in an area that is low on rentals and it can be rented 30 times a year fairly easily. Maybe the rental rate can be adjusted a little bit by upgrading a few things in the condo. Maybe you can lower some unnecessary expenses.

You should be warned not to fall so in love with a property that you are willing to look past the fact that it doesn't fit the formula well at all. Of course, this is only important if you are looking at the property as an investment.

Chapter Summary

In this chapter I tried to show you how easy it is to find potential properties for purchase. Whether it is via the internet, a broker, or word of mouth, finding a property for sale in the Dominican Republic is not a difficult task.

Once you have located a few properties that meet your initial criteria such as location, size, price, I have given you a good formula to see if these properties fit into. In a nutshell the formula is; If your monthly mortgage payment is less than or equal to one peak week rental, and you rent approximately 17 weeks per year, you will break even. I also gave you some things to consider even if the property appears to either fit into the formula, or if it fails to meet the formula guidelines. Remember to consider things like: How often can you get this property rented? Are rental rates in this area increasing or decreasing? What are some of the costs that may go up or down?

Once you have found a property, and assuming it meets the criteria of the formula then it's time to negotiate the purchase of the property with the seller.

Chapter 8

The Process of Purchasing From Negotiation to Closing

If you have thoroughly followed the advice of the last chapter on evaluating potential properties then you have already won half the battle. It is entirely important that you come to the negotiation table completely prepared.

The most important things that you should know about the property before you make your offer are:

1. Does it fit into my formula? I have given you a good formula, now you have to use it. Remember, all though the formula is flexible, it is not wise to purchase an investment property if it falls too far out of this formula. You'll be losing money every month. Yes there is a chance you will make it up with eventual appreciation, but that is speculating, not investing.
2. Have I evaluated all the necessary documents to see if the property achieves the income that the owner has stated? Below I have given you a list of what some of these documents are. Make sure that you get them. Don't let an anxious broker talk you out of thoroughly reviewing all relevant information. You're the one buying the property, not them.
3. Do I know the owner's motivation for selling? This is important because the more eager the owner is to sell the better position you are in at the negotiation table.
4. Have I conducted a preliminary inspection? Have you physically walked through the property? If there are issues that need to be resolved that is beyond your ability have you had the required professional view the property?

5. Have I compared the property with other real estate in the area? The more confident you are about the market value of a property the more prepared you will be to offer and counter offer.
6. Have I picked the broker's brain to make sure I know everything he knows about this property? Sometimes a less than honest broker will withhold information unless directly asked. Make sure you ask as many questions about this property as you can. Don't feel like you're being a pest. Chances are this sale will make him quite a bit of money, so don't feel bad.
7. Have I determined the price that I'm willing to pay? Set a limit on how much you are willing to spend on this property.
8. Have I found two or three properties that I'm interested in so that I'm in a better mind set for negotiation? Sometimes a novice investor gets caught up in the chase and agrees to pay more for a property so as to not lose the deal. You can limit the chance of this happening by having other properties lined up if this deal falls through.

If you are unsure of exactly what kind of data you should be asking the owner for I have included some of the more common documentation about the property. The list includes, but is not limited to:

- Lot number and area of land
- Survey or detailed diagram of property, showing any borders and structures on the property
- Building size and age
- Zoning regulation for area
- Real estate tax, insurance, and other expense data
- Full rental report on property
- Complete list of people currently employed to work at the property. This list includes maids, groundskeepers, security guards, pool cleaners, etc.

Negotiating

To negotiate is simply to, "find a price agreed to by a willing buyer and a willing seller in an arm's length transaction, without undue pressure on either side." An arm's length means that there are other parties there to witness the transaction. It also implies that there was no force by either party leading to the sale.

Once you have a realistic target price, and most brokers will let you know if you offer is "in the ballpark," you can begin the negotiation process.

A basic guideline for negotiation

1. Compare the price you'd like to pay to the price the seller is asking.
2. Offer roughly 10 percent less than your target price.
3. If the seller counteroffers with a reduction in their asking price, raise your offer closer to your target price.

The negotiation phase is the time you put your game face on. The seller and broker must believe that you cannot be swindled into paying a higher price than you initially were prepared to pay. The more research you have done and the more comfortable you are with your position, the more seriously the seller will take you. It should be made known that you have gathered enough information to set a value on the property, and if the seller's price doesn't match that value, then you are willing to walk away from the transaction.

Your broker's role in the negotiation process

Since you will more than likely be using a broker to secure an investment in the Dominican Republic, you should have an idea of what their roles will be in the negotiation process.

1. They will make the original offer on your behalf.
2. They will then relay the seller's counteroffer to you.
3. They will then allow you time to consider.
4. They will play the role of mediator trying to convince both of you that the offer's offer is legit and should be taken seriously.

Contract of Sale

Once the two parties have formally agreed to a set price and terms for the property it is time to write up a contract of sale. All of your homework should really have been done before you signed the contract of sale, but you should still have your lawyer include a time limit for you to inspect the property again. If you are purchasing raw land that you plan to build on, then now is the time to start talking to engineers and architects to give you reports.

Usually the seller's attorney will write the contract of sale (which must be notarized to be considered legal in the Dominican.) In a later section I will list more specifics, but the contract usually comprises:

- The property address and legal descriptions of the property.
- Agreed upon price and terms (all cash or subject to financing).
- A financing contingency clause; that is how much time the buyer has to secure a loan. Most clauses have a deadline for a buyer to produce a loan commitment, usually no more than three months.
- An inspection contingency clause- how much time the buyer has to physically inspect the property. If it is raw land or commercial property this includes getting necessary permits needed for building or running a particular business.
- The amount of the good faith deposit, or down payment, on contract. Usually this amount is 10 percent. The good faith money is held in escrow by the seller's attorney or title insurance company until the closing of the transaction.

Inspection contingencies

The deadline for the formal inspection of the property and its accompanying books and records is usually within 30 days following the signing of the contract of sale. If the property does not pass inspection, or unexpected problems are found, one of three things may happen.

1. They buyer may withdraw from the transaction and get the escrow deposit back.
2. The seller may agree to correct the problem, and extend the closing date.
3. The buyer and seller may agree to an adjustment of price. Of course, if the buyer is trying to secure financing, the bank would also have to agree.

Financing Contingencies

I know that in the United States most contracts contain a financing contingency. Because of the fact that financing is different in every country, you may not always receive this contingency when purchasing in the DR. In general though, a formal loan commitment by a lending institution may take 30-90 days. Usually when you sign the contract, you will have already secured an informal agreement from a mortgage broker, but getting a formal loan agreement takes time. The financing contingency states the parameters, or terms, under which the buyer is willing to borrow. For example, "subject to 70 percent financing at an interest rate of 8 to 9 percent."

If you, the buyer, cannot get a loan according to the financing contingency terms, you have the right to terminate the contract and get your money back. You may also be able to withdraw from the deal if you cannot get a formal financing commitment from a financial institution before the financing deadline. In addition to the contingency clauses and related deadline dates, the closing date is also set in the contract of sale, usually for 30 days after the last deadline has been met.

Loss of deposit

You have to make sure that you notify the seller of any problems that you have with any of the contingencies. If you or your attorney doesn't notify them it will be assumed that there aren't any. If later on you try to get out of the contract, you will probably lose your good faith deposit. You should also make sure the terms of this happening are spelled out in the contract.

It is only fair that you forfeit your deposit if you fail to notify the seller of any inspection or financing problems, because after you've signed the contract, the seller has:

- Taken the property off the market for a period of time. He or she is prohibited from selling the property to anyone else.

- Have been subject to legal fees and other costs dealing with the prospective buyer.

The only things that can usually get you out of the contract without facing the penalty of losing your deposit are:

- Your engineer found severe problems with property, including environmental issues.
- You couldn't get a loan from a lender with the terms stated in the contract.

Financing Your Dominican Republic Real Estate Investment

It is very easy to take a trip down to the Dominican Republic, wander the streets, eat in the restaurants, mingle with the locals, bathe on the beach, and decide that you want to own property down there. Hell…that is probably how this whole thing started for most of you reading this book. You went there on vacation, fell in love with the place, and then did some research and found out that there is a real estate market down there set to explode. And in that moment you decided that the reward was much greater than the risk, and that you were not going to let this opportunity to pass you by.

It amazes me that in the frenzy of the decision to go ahead and follow a dream, most people neglect to figure out exactly how they are going to pay for their new villa, condo, hotel, or pristine piece of ocean front land.

I deal with many people looking to buy in the Dominican Republic on a daily basis. I would say that about 10% of the people looking to make an investment in real estate down there have the cash on hand to make the purchase. Does this make their lives easier? It sure makes the process of buying easier. But it doesn't necessarily mean that it is the smarter way to go.

There is a saying amongst real estate investors that the average person has no problem racking up thousands of dollars of debt on personal possessions, but is scared senseless to use debt for improving a business, or investing in real estate which will sit in the asset column.

The accomplished investor knows that going into debt is almost prerequisite to being rich. The key is to going into debt to purchase assets that will either bring in a positive cash flow, or appreciate at a rate that far exceeds the current financing rates.

We learned in that chapter six that debt or leverage was one of the three profit sources of real estate investments. Here is a brief recap of how it works:

Leverage

Our second example of appreciation will include the third source of profit from real estate transactions: effects of leverage or borrowed funds. We'll again use the $200,000 Samana condo with $150,000 loan at 8%, and for simplification we'll ignore the effects of amortization of the loan.

Now let's look at our example. Here to you've held the property for 10 years:

Price of property (initially)	$200,000
Mortgage	$150,000
Down payment	$50,000
Original cash flow	$20,000 per year
Future cash flow	$40,000 per year
Average cash flow	$30,000 per year
Less interest on $150,000 at 8%	($12,000)
Average cash flow after interest	($18,000)

After 10 years

Value of property	$400,000
Mortgage (assuming no pay down of principle)	$150,000
Net Equity	$250,000

Plus 10-year cash flow

Average annual income	$30,000
Less annual interest	($12,000)
Net annual cash flow	$18,000
Cash flow over 10 years	$180,000
Total after 10 years	$430,000
Original cash investment	$ 50,000

Our original cash investment of $50,000 increased to $430,000 in just 10 years. This is an example of well located condo in a booming area. The numbers show how much potential there is.

So as you can see just because you may have the cash to purchase your investment free and clear doesn't necessarily mean that you should.

That brings us to the all important question: *How do I go about getting financing for a property in the Dominican Republic?*

The answer to that question, unfortunately, is not cut and dry. There are many variables as to what kind of financing is available. One of the main influences in what kind of financing is available is your current location. Financing options vary from country to country, and even vary from state to state here in the United States.

What I am going to do in this chapter is give you a good over view of what kinds of financing you should be looking into. What is important is to know that when it comes to financing a real estate investment there is always more than one option. It is my goal in this chapter to make sure that you explore all available options before committing to anything.

Exploring Your Financing Options

In this next section I am going to give you a brief introduction to many different financing programs available at the moment. Will all of these programs be available to you? Probably not. Like I said earlier, different countries, different states offer different financing programs. Your financing program will also be affected by your job, income, equity in your current home, credit history, and so on. It is my purpose to familiarize you with several programs to give you a foundation to begin your search for financing. Any terms and rates I quote throughout this chapter are subject to change as the finance market is constantly changing.

Using a Bank in the Dominican Republic

In the Dominican Republic, financing, as in many countries outside North America and Europe is seldom available as you are accustomed. The majority of purchases are cash in full.

In the past it was very difficult to get financing in the Dominican Republic, and if you could find it you were usually looking at local mortgage rates running 20% per annum.

But things are changing rapidly in the Dominican Republic as the country wants to encourage as much investment as possible. Your options are ever increasing in regards to how you can go about purchasing your property.

One way would be to talk to one of the Banks down there, when in the country. The Banks will consider lending up to around 80% on the purchase price subject to their terms and conditions. Loans are available on land, villas, apartments and construction. No lower limit to the amount loaned.

The Bank will need insurance on both the property and the borrowers' lives. Proof of income needed, in any currency. Total time needed from completing documents to receiving loan: 3 – 4 weeks. Interest rates are around 9.5% and it should be noted the borrower pays the Bank legal fees.

What is Available?

Fixed DR 15-Year Program
• Interest rate fixed for 5-year U.S. dollar loan
• Amortized over 15-years
• Structured as an adjustment off of the FHLB (currently at 5.3%). Adjustment is 3.5%. (This is currently and effective interest rate of 8.8%)
• Maximum loan-to-value is 70%

• Maximum loan amount is $1,250,000.00
Fixed DR 20-Year Program
• Interest rate fixed for 10-year U.S. dollar loan
• Amortized over 20-years
• Structured as an adjustment off of the FHLB (currently at 5.3%). Adjustment is 4.0%. (This is currently and effective interest rate of 9.3%)
• Maximum loan-to-value is 70%
• Maximum loan amount is $1,250,000.00

Variable DR 20-Year Program
• Variable 20-year U.S. dollar loan
• Amortized over 20-years
• Structured as an adjustable rate mortgage with a start rate of 8.5%
• 2.0% rate cap and the loan adjusts annually
• Maximum loan-to-value is 70%
• Maximum loan amount is $2,000,000.00
Exceptions to both loan-to-value and loan amount are given on a case by case basis.

What Do You Need?
The documentation required to obtain a Dominican Republic mortgage is similar to what's needed in Canada, the UK or the United States. Lenders are looking for the following:
• 2-years of personal income confirmation (employment letters, income tax forms, Notice of Assessment (Canada))
• If self-employed, 2-years of corporate financial statements
• Consent to obtain your credit report(s)
• Confirmation and source of your down payment

What are My Costs?

There is a one-time placement fee of 5% of the mortgage value. This 5% can be added on to the mortgage balance. In addition, there will be an appraisal required to determine the property's value. This will be approximately $500.00.

Second Home Mortgage from Your Home Country

This is one of the most ideal ways to purchase a vacation home in the Dominican Republic. What is great about these loans is the fact that you are not penalized in any way for purchasing a second home. This type of mortgage is basically the same as if you were applying for a home loan.

Because you are not facing any penalties for purchasing a home loan the guidelines are similar to qualifying for a home mortgage. You must be able to afford this second home along with your current home based on your financial statement.

Since you are declaring it as a second home and not an investment property there is no consideration for the potential income it will bring. It is also important to make sure that if you plan on renting the property that there are no restrictions in the mortgage that will prevent you from doing so.

If you are interested in this type of mortgage the best person to talk to is a local loan officer. It is a loan officer's job to match a potential buyer with the best program available to them. These people work for commission so it is in their best interest to diligently search for a program that will allow you to make the purchase. But you have to remember that not all loan officers will be familiar with overseas purchasing so it is important to talk to several before you make any kind of obligation.

A suggestion to help give you the extra edge is to use the leverage tool of combining a seventy-five percent first mortgage with a ten percent down payment and ask the seller to carry back fifteen percent of the purchase price in seller financing or obtain a second mortgage from the lender. This is possible to do as the secondary market that purchases second-home loans will allow you to sidestep private mortgage insurance (PMI) for the simple reason that your first mortgage is less than the eighty percent loan generally requiring PMI. As well you can most likely save some money on interest by choosing a seventy-five percent loan over an eighty percent and negotiating the repayment terms with the seller.

Although the mortgage market is constantly changing, one company that offers a program of interest in the east coast of the United States is Aceltis Financial Group. They currently offer up to 70% financing on properties in the

Dominican Republic. Their contact information can be found at the back of this book.

Here is a sample of some of the terms being offered on Dominican real estate:

Basic Terms

- Minimum residential mortgage loan $100,000 US
- Maximum residential mortgage loan $10,000,000 US
- Interest rates 7-10% fixed, depending on borrower's individual qualifications
- 20- to 30-year amortization, with 5- to 10-year balloons
- Target LTV 80%; in some cases we can get a CLTV as high as 100%
- Commercial/development financing for development projects; $5m US minimum, no maximum.
- Even for prospective buyers with less-than-perfect credit history and weaker financial, there is also have financing available at somewhat higher rates, typically 12-15%.
- All-inclusive financing for purchase and/or construction (i.e., "construction-to-permanent" financing): These funds can be used for purchase of an existing home/condo, or for purchase of land and construction of a home on that lot. Construction funding may be disbursed in a single draw, or in multiple phases.

Here are some more terms being offered to US citizens on overseas Real estate:

- The "American-style" mortgage trust loan program is currently available to home-buyers at selected resorts and residential development projects.
- By leveraging U.S. assets, this program provides affordable permanent mortgage loans when local bank financing would otherwise be unaffordable or unavailable.
- This is different from a home equity loan and your US assets are freed and returned after a period of seasoning usually 10 to 12 months.
- Must be a U.S. citizen with U.S. assets, and net worth of at least the value of the vacation/retirement property.

- Loan amounts: $150,000 to $2,500,000 USD
- 20- to 30-year amortization
- Interest rates: 7% to 9% fixed, depending upon creditworthiness
- 70% Loan to value
- Full-document loans; stated loans possible; loans are in U.S. dollars
- Construction to permanent financing and undeveloped land financing available

Required Documentation

✓ Completed and signed borrower application (Form 1003) including complete list of real estate owned.
✓ Authorization to check credit
✓ Completed and signed service agreement and disclosures
✓ Proof of income—Salary employee: W-2s for previous 2 years; complete 2 years of tax returns; last 2 pay stubs; full verification of employment, work telephone number
✓ Proof of income—Self-employed: Complete 2 years of tax returns; CPA letter and/or reference letters, or other business documentation
✓ Proof of other income, such as rental income or fixed income: Rental agreements or tax returns to support other income
✓ Most recent monthly account statement from each mortgage account or asset account
✓ Purchase Agreement

Investor Mortgage

In this type of mortgage the bank is well aware that you are buying this property strictly as an investment. When deciding whether or not to issue you financing the bank will look at the rental history of the property along with your current financial picture.

Because these loans are considered a higher risk you are looking at a higher interest rate, and higher fees.

These loans should also be discussed with your local loan officer.

Fixed Rate, Fixed Term

The most popular type of mortgage is a fixed rate. These mortgages are so popular because everything is set up front and stays constant throughout the life of the loan. With these loans your interest rate and monthly payments never change.

These mortgages are available for 30 years, 20 years, 15 years, and even 10 years. In these kinds of loans a big chunk of the monthly payment goes towards paying off the interest. As the loan is paid down more of the monthly payment goes towards the principle. A typical 30 year fixed-rate mortgage takes 22.5 years of level payments to pay half of the original amount.

Usually when you are purchasing an investment property you will want to amortize the loan over the longest time possible. This will keep the monthly payments as low as possible and allow you to achieve a positive cash flow on a monthly basis.

Interest Only Loans

Another option that is popular for "short term" owners are interest only loans. With an interest loan your monthly payment consists solely of your interest payment on the loan. Although by paying interest only you are able to keep your monthly payment at a minimum, you are not paying down the principle balance.

These loans are usually spread out over 5-10 years with the entire balance due in a balloon payment at the end of the term. Sometimes you have the option of refinancing into a conventional mortgage at a certain percentage point above prime.

This is a program that is best suited for people looking to purchase a property and then resell, or flip, the property a short time later. Because your monthly payment is less than it would be with a conventional mortgage it allows you to purchase a more expensive property. This is an ideal mortgage if you believe that you are purchasing a property that will rise in value quickly over the next five years.

The drawback is that you can never reliably predict what will happen to the value of a property. If you purchase a property with this type of loan and proceed to make interest only payments over the next five years, your balance on the loan will be the same at the end of the five years. If the property market took a turn for the worse, you may be in a difficult position if you own a property with a mortgage balance greater than its value.

Self-directed IRA

If the option of using tax-deferred funds to purchase property sounds appealing, you'll need to locate an independent IRA custodian that allows real estate investments and work with that company to set up an IRA account. Most banks and brokerage companies—the most common IRA account options—limit your choices to certificates of deposit, stocks, mutual funds, annuities, and similar financial instruments. But Section 408 of the Internal Revenue Code permits individuals to purchase land, commercial property, condominiums, residential property, trust deeds, or real estate contracts with funds held in many common forms of IRAs, including a traditional IRA, a Roth IRA , and a Simplified Employee Pension plan, or SEP-IRA.

To find a custodian that specializes in real estate, search under terms such as "real estate IRA" or "self-directed IRA." This latter term was coined by the financial industry in the 1980s to distinguish the self-directed IRA from other IRAs that focus on stocks and bonds. The IRA account holder can't serve as the custodian of his or her own account. However, it's important to select a custodian knowledgeable about the types of investment you're interested in, because the custodian holds title to the real estate. Do your homework, and understand what you're getting into.

Fees can vary widely among custodians, as can the flexibility of the services provided for account holders. If the custodian holds real estate on your behalf, but does not service it (collect the rent, etc.), you may have to contract with other providers. However, be sure that all rents are paid into the IRA and that all taxes are paid by the IRA.

Purchasing the Property

Most IRA custodians that hold real estate will usually allow you to purchase raw or vacant land, residential properties, or commercial buildings for your portfolio. In addition, some custodians may permit foreign property or leveraged property.

Since buying a property may require more funds than you currently have available in your IRA, you also can have your IRA purchase an interest in the property in conjunction with other individuals, such as a spouse, business associate, or friend. Also keep in mind that if the property is leveraged, the debt must be a non-recourse promissory note.

Unfortunately, Internal Revenue Service regulations will not let you use the real estate owned by your IRA as your residence or vacation home. Nor can your business lease space in your IRA-held property. The underlying premise for any real estate investment purchased with IRA funds is that you can't have any personal use or benefit of the property. To do so may cost you plenty in taxes and penalties.

There are a few other IRS limitations as well. You cannot place a real estate property that you already own into your IRA. Your spouse, your parents, or your children also couldn't have owned the property before it was purchased by your IRA. Property owned by siblings may be allowed, since the Internal Revenue Code (section 4975) specifies that only "lineal descendents" be disqualified.

Once you've chosen a property, your IRA custodian—not you personally—must actually purchase it. The title will reflect the name of your IRA custodian for your benefit (such as Silver Trust Co., Custodian FBO John Doe IRA). In addition, if you put up earnest money with your personal funds, you'll need to make sure you include that amount in the total due so that the title company can reimburse you upon closing.

Operating an IRA-held Property

Because all property expenses, including taxes, insurance, and repairs, must be paid from funds in your IRA, you'll need liquid funds available in your account. Of course, all income generated from the property will be deposited in your IRA account so you can use that money to cover your costs. You also can make annual contributions within federal guidelines.

Currently, you can contribute $3,000 annually to a traditional or Roth IRA ($3,500 if you're age 50 or older) and as much as 15 percent of your annual compensation, up to $40,000, if you're a self-employed individual with a SEP-IRA. If your account doesn't have funds to cover property expenses, you will have to withdraw the property from your IRA and pay taxes on the value of the property, as well as possible penalties for early withdrawal.

It's also possible to sell properties while they are held by your IRA, so long as the purchaser is not a family member. Once a deal closes, your IRA account now holds the cash proceeds—ready for you to make your next investment. An alternative is to sell an IRA-held property with seller financing so that all payments made by the buyers are paid to the IRA.

Distributing Your Property

You can withdraw real estate from your IRA and use it as a residence or second home when you reach retirement age (age 59½ or older for a penalty-free withdrawal). At that time, you can elect either to have the IRA sell the property or take an in-kind distribution of the property. Under that arrangement, your IRA custodian assigns the title to the property to you. You will then have to pay income taxes on the current value of the property if it's been held in a traditional IRA. If the property was held in a Roth IRA, you won't owe taxes at distribution. This makes a Roth IRA extremely attractive if you anticipate that your real estate investments will appreciate over time.

Whether your retirement strategy is to hold properties or buy and sell for gain, real estate investing through your IRA can yield extraordinary returns toward your future retirement.

IRA Options

While any form of IRA allows for real estate investment, there are other pluses and minuses to consider when choosing the account type that's best for you:

- A **traditional IRA** lets you deduct annual contributions (currently set at $3,000, or $3,500 if you're age 50 or older) from your income. However, once you begin withdrawing money, those funds will be taxed as regular income.

- A **Roth IRA** gives you no deduction on your current contributions (again $3,000), but does allow you to withdraw funds tax-free. If you expect to buy a real estate investment in an IRA and hold it for a long period, this is probably your best option, particularly if the property increases in value over that period.

- A **SEP-IRA** is designed for self-employed individuals and small companies. You can contribute up to 25 percent of your compensation, or $40,000, whichever is less. However, keep in mind that if you have employees, you must make contributions for them as well. This option is a great alternative for real estate practitioners who can make the higher contributions because they can build up funds more rapidly to purchase properties. Withdrawals from a SEP-IRA are treated like those of a traditional IRA for tax purposes.

As you can see there are many options for financing your property in the Dominican Republic. Just as I said that it was important for you to do research on the different areas and the different types of properties, I believe that it is just as important for you to thoroughly research all of your available financing options.

Here in the United States the financial market is ever changing. Programs that were available yesterday cannot be guaranteed to be available today. That is why it is important to have a knowledgeable broker working with you. The last thing you want to do is plan your purchase with a program that is no longer available.

Another smart thing to do if you plan on using bank financing is to get pre qualified from a bank. This means that once you've determined what kind of property you intend on buying, and have set a limit for what you intend on spending, begin shopping for a loan. This way you are in a much better position to close quickly than if you wait until after putting an offer on a property to head to the bank.

Having your financing in place ahead of time also puts you in a better place at the bargaining table. If you are making an offer, and can show the seller that you have financing already available, you offer will be taken more seriously than a buyer who comes to the table unprepared. This may allow you to offer a little less and still walk away with the property.

I don't want you to get overwhelmed with the financing aspect of purchasing a property. There are plenty of qualified brokers out there who would be happy to sit down with you and go over all the different programs that are available in your market. In the index of this book I have listed several of the companies that are well known for supplying financing for investors looking to purchase in the Dominican.

The legal Process of Purchasing Real Estate Specifically in the Dominican Republic

Real estate transactions in the Dominican Republic are governed by Property Registry Law No. 108-05 and its Regulations, in force since April 4, 2007. Ownership of property is documented by "Certificates of Title" issued by Title Registry Offices.

The Steps

Preliminary Steps

Real estate purchases in the Dominican Republic do not usually follow the North American pattern of a written offer tendered by the buyer to the seller, followed by the seller's written acceptance. Instead, after verbal agreement is reached by the buyer and seller on the price, a binding

Promise of Sale is prepared by an attorney (solicitor) or notary public who is signed by both parties. (Notaries in the Dominican Republic are required to have a law degree.)

- Because you are unfamiliar with Dominican laws I highly recommend that you obtain the services of a real estate attorney before signing any documents or making any deposits. Depending on what you and the seller agree on, your attorney may proceed with the due diligence first, before preparing the promise of sale, or he can prepare the promise of sale first, and include the due diligence as an inspection clause as we discussed earlier.

Promise of Sale

This is a formal document, binding on both parties, and signed by them in the presence of a Notary Public. From a practical point of view, it is more important than the Deed of Sale, since it generally contains a complete and detailed description of the entire transaction up to the time when the purchase price has been paid in full and the property is ready to be conveyed to the buyer. A well-drafted Promise of Sale should contain at least the following provisions:

- ✓ Full name and particulars of the parties. If the seller is married, the spouse must also sign.
- ✓ Legal description of the property to be purchased.
- ✓ Purchase price and payment terms.
- ✓ Default clause.
- ✓ Date of delivery of the property.
- ✓ Due diligence required or done.
- ✓ Representations by the seller and remedies in case of misrepresentation.
- ✓ Obligation by seller of signing the Deed of Sale upon receipt of final payment.

* Many attorneys (solicitors) and notaries in the Dominican Republic do not protect the buyer adequately in the Promise of Sale. Among the most common deficiencies are the following:

- The buyer is allowed to pay a large percentage of the price of sale without any security or direct interest over the property. In case of misuse of these funds, the buyer's remedies may be limited to suing the seller personally. Many condo buyers in Santo Domingo have suffered through this experience in the last few years. Generally, the developer uses the buyers' funds, along with a bank loan, to finance the construction. The bank collaterizes the loan with a mortgage on the property. If the developer runs into financial difficulties or misappropriates the funds, the bank forecloses and the buyers lose both their money and "their" property.

- Payments are not conditioned on the availability of clear title or the adequate progress of construction. Sellers, therefore, may demand payment or place the buyer in default without performing their own basic obligations.

- Escrow agents are rarely used. The seller, therefore, has control over the funds as they are paid.

Deed of Sale ("Contrato de Venta")

This is also a formal document binding on both parties, and signed by them in the presence of a Notary Public. It is used primarily for the purpose of conveying the property from the seller to the buyer. (In case of a cash purchase, it is simpler and cheaper to go directly from verbal negotiations to the signing of a "Contrato de Venta", instead of taking the preliminary step of signing a Promise of Sale.)

Determination and Payment of Transfer and Registry Taxes

The authenticated Deed of Sale is taken to the nearest Internal Revenue Office where a request is made for the appraisal of the property. The Internal Revenue Office checks if the seller is in compliance with his tax obligations and selects an inspector to do the appraisal. The determination of the amount of taxes to be paid may take a few days or weeks, depending on the availability of the property inspector.

Filing at the Registry of Title

Once the property has been appraised and taxes paid, the Deed of Sale and the Certificate of Title of the seller are deposited, along with the documentation provided by Internal Revenue, at the Title Registry Office for the jurisdiction where the property is located.

Certificate of Title

At the Title Registry Office, the sale is recorded and a new Certificate of Title is issued in the name of the buyer. The property belongs to the buyer from the time the sale is recorded at the Registry. The time for the issuance of the new Certificate of Title may vary from a few days to a few months depending on the Title Registry Office where the sale was recorded.

Due Diligence

Many attorneys (solicitors) in the Dominican Republic do not perform the required due diligence on real estate transactions, limiting themselves in many cases to obtaining a certification on the status of the property from the Title Registry Office. It often happens that the real estate agent and/or the seller pressure the buyer into a hurried closing despite the advice of legal counsel.

To start the due diligence, the seller should provide the buyer or the attorney with the following documents:

- ✓ Copy of the Certificate of Title to the property.

- ✓ Copy of the official survey to the property or plat plan. Under the new Property Registry Law, the sale of properties without a government-approved plat ("deslinde") cannot be recorded at the Registry, except in the following cases: (1) Sales executed before April 4, 2007, which may be recorded during a two-year period ending on April 4, 2009, and (2) Sales of the entire property executed after April 4, 2007 (sales of portions are not allowed), for just one time.

- ✓ Copy of his or her identification card ("Cédula") or Passport and that of the spouse, if married.

114

✓ Copy of the receipt showing the last property tax payment (IPI) or copy of the certificate stating that the property is exempt from property tax, and certification from the Internal Revenue Office showing the seller is current with his or her tax obligations.

If the seller is a corporation:

✓ Copy of the corporate documentation, including bylaws, up-to-date registration at the Mercantile Registry and resolution authorizing the sale.

✓ Certification from the Internal Revenue Office showing the corporation is current with its tax obligations, especially Income Tax and Tax on Assets.

If the seller is part of a condominium:

✓ Copy of the condominium declaration.

✓ Copy of the condominium regulations.

✓ Copy of the approved construction plans.

✓ Certification from the condominium administration showing the seller is current with his or her condo dues.

✓ Copies of the minutes of the last three condominium meetings.

If the property is a house:

✓ Copy of the approved construction plans.

✓ Inventory of furniture, etc.

✓ Copies of the utilities contracts and receipts showing that the seller is current.

Once the documentation listed above is obtained, the attorney should address every item on the following checklist:

✓ Title Search: A certification should be obtained from the appropriate Title Registry Office regarding the status of the property, stating who the owner is and whether any mortgages, liens or encumbrances affect it. The buyer should insist that his or her attorney confirm the results of the Registrar's search by investigating the pertinent files at the Title Registry Office.

✓ Survey: An independent surveyor should verify that the property to be sold coincides with the one shown on the survey presented by the seller except when the property is located in a previously inspected subdivision. Cases have occurred in which a buyer acquires title over a property some distance away from the one he or she believes to be purchasing due to careless work by a previous surveyor or to fraud by the seller. The survey should be checked even when the seller provides a government-approved plat.

✓ Inspection of Improvements: A qualified builder or architect should examine any improvements to be sold (house, condo) to confirm that the plans presented are correct and that the improvements are in good condition.

✓ Permits: The attorney should confirm that the property to be purchased may be used for the purposes sought by the buyer. There are many legal restrictions which should be taken into account before purchasing. For example, Law 305 of 1968 establishes a 60-meter "maritime zone" along the entire Dominican coastline, measured from the high tide mark inland, which in effect converts all beaches into public property. No building is allowed within the maritime zone without a special permit from the Executive Branch. Also, in tourist areas, there are building restrictions administered by the Ministry of Tourism.

✓ Possession: The attorney should check that the seller is in possession of the property. It should be ensured that no squatters' rights of any kind exist. Special precautions should be taken with unfenced properties outside known subdivisions. Fencing them before closing is advisable. If there are tenants on the property, the buyer should be informed that Dominican law is protective of a tenant's rights and that evicting a recalcitrant tenant is time-consuming and expensive.

✓ Employees: The seller should pay any employees working on the property their legal severance; otherwise the buyer may find himself liable for the payment later.

✓ Utilities: The attorney or buyer should check that the seller does not have any utility bills pending by enquiring at the appropriate power distributor, water, cable, and telephone companies.

Taxes and Expenses on Property Transfers

Taxes must be paid before filing the purchase at the Title Registry Office. Taxes and expenses on the conveyance of real estate are approximately 4.4% of the government-appraised value of the property, soon to be raised to 6.4%, as follows:

- 3% Transfer Tax (Law # 288-04)

- 1.3% Document Stamp Tax (Law # 835-45) (Actually, RD$232 pesos for the first RD$20,000 pesos and 13 per thousand for the rest).

- 2% Registry Tax (Law #108-05), applicable to properties valued at RD$5 million pesos or more, which will come into effect sometime in the near future upon creation of the Indemnity Fund established by the Law.

- Minor expenses such as tax on certified check, sundry stamps and tips at the Registry.

Taxes are paid based on the market value of the property as determined by the tax authorities, not on the price of purchase stated in the deed of sale. Buyers wishing to lessen the impact of transfer taxes have the option of using a loophole in the law which allows the contribution in kind of property into corporations without paying transfer taxes. For this, cooperation from the seller is essential.

Property Taxes

Properties held in the name of an individual are subject to an annual property tax ("IPI") of 1% of government-appraised value in excess of RD$5,000,000 pesos except for un-built lots or farms outside city limits and properties whose owner is 65 years old or older, who has registered it in his or her name for more than 15 years and has no other property.

If the property is held by a corporation, no property tax is due. Instead, the corporation must pay a 1% tax on corporate asset. However, any income tax paid by the corporation will constitute a credit toward the tax on assets, so that if corporate income taxes paid are equal to or higher than the taxes on assets due, the corporation will have no obligation to pay taxes on its assets.

Title Insurance

In the Dominican Republic, as in many Latin American and European countries, the government provides title insurance. The old Land Registry Law established an indemnity fund with which to pay claimants who due, for example, to an error of the Registrar, were deprived of their property. Unfortunately, the funds collected were used by the government for other purposes.
The Property Registry Law in effect since April 4, 2007, has created a new 2% tax on all conveyances in order to establish an indemnity fund. It is also possible to obtain title insurance from private insurers.

Purchase of Real Estate By Foreigners

There are no restrictions on foreigners purchasing real property in the Dominican Republic. Formerly, Decree 2543 of March 22, 1945 and its amendments required that foreigners obtain prior Presidential approval except in certain cases. Decree 21-98 of January 8, 1998 abolished this regulation and established as the only requirement that the Title Registry Offices keep a record, for statistical purposes, of all purchases made by foreigners.

Inheritance of Real Estate by Foreigners

There are no restrictions on foreigners inheriting title to real property in the Dominican Republic. Inheritance taxes have been recently lowered to 3% of the appraised value of the estate. If the beneficiary resides outside the Dominican Republic, inheritance taxes are subject to a 50% surcharge, raising the tax rate to 4.5%.
Inheritance of real estate is governed by Dominican law which provides for "forced heirship": part of the inheritance must go to certain heirs by law.

For example, a foreigner with a child must reserve 50% of the estate to that child despite the existence of a will or of the law of his country of residence. To avoid the application of Dominican rules of inheritance to the estate, it is advisable for foreigners to hold real estate indirectly through a holding company.

Things to be aware of

Upon arrival in the Dominican Republic, you may see places that advertise properties around the particular destination you are visiting. Be careful to take the time to investigate properties all over the area you are interested in, as properties that are advertised do not necessarily reflect the true market value of all available properties. Knowing how real estate purchases work in the Dominican Republic, what's involved, the other costs that may be associated, what questions to ask, etc., will help ensure you make an informed purchase decision.

You may hear that when a foreigner purchases property in the Dominican Republic, there are no annual real estate taxes and/or no title transfer taxes. Neither of these statements are completely true. Depending on the property purchased, as well as how it is purchased, there may or may not be an annual real estate tax liability and a title transfer tax. There are situations where tax exemption can occur, but it is important to find out where this is legally the case. The best thing to do is to speak with Real Estate Agents/Agencies or Attorneys/Law Offices to learn what your options are for the particular property you are interested in purchasing.

If you decide to purchase directly from the owner, there are some things that you should keep in mind. There is no real estate or governmental body that sends real estate and property tax reminders to owners if these fees have not been paid. If an owner does not pay these dues, the government will ensure they collect any arrears at the time of sale, if not up to an additional 50% penalty on these arrears as well, before enabling the title of the property to be transferred. This could prevent the sale from happening if the seller does not have the money to pay these arrears (and any penalties), or, depending on what has already been transacted between the buyer and the seller, put the buyer in a position to pay any outstanding dues before obtaining title of the property. To prevent this from happening, ask the seller to provide proof of the previous tax payments that have been made on the property.

A seller should always be able to provide you with at least a photocopy of the title to the property so that you can verify with the titles office that the title is good and that there are no liens against the property. It is also wise to have the seller provide a recent copy of the tax assessment of the property, matching it against the title to ensure it fully describes the property and all of its buildings. If the title office has only registered the piece of land, and a home or building was built afterwards without being registered, you could be liable for the arrears in taxes on this home or building since it was built.

If you are looking into purchasing a new residential property, the developer may not be able to provide you with anything but a photocopy of the 'master title' for the entire development. This is okay, but you will need to also complete a 'contract of sale' if you decide to purchase, to make your purchase legal and binding. Ensure the 'contract of sale' is notarized by an Attorney and is filed properly with the applicable department. Once the entire project is completed, the developer cancels the 'master title' in exchange for providing individual land titles to each of the project's buyers. Once the development is completed, the developer should provide you and all other buyers with an individual land title for your portion of the project, but to be sure, at the time of sale, along with the 'contract of sale', you should get an agreement in writing from the developer stating he will provide your individual land title in no longer than one year's time. If the developer is unwilling to do so, you should be skeptical about buying the property.

If you are a first time buyer in the Dominican Republic, it would probably be in your best interest to gain the assistance of a Real Estate Agents/Agencies or Attorneys/Law Offices to assist you with your purchase to ensure all of the particulars have been addressed in order to avoid future surprises.

Chapter 8
Forming a Dominican Corporation

Why Form a Dominican Company?
.

Like any other strategy to protect your assets and gain tax advantages, the main goal of asset protection is the separation of personal property from the beneficial owner. In other words, if your assets are not in your name, they cannot be taken away from you if a lawsuit arises or if someone wishes to attach your property for some reason. In essence you do not own the property, a completely separate entity does. But this is not the only real benefit of a Dominican Company. Owning your Dominican Republic Vacation property, real estate or investments via an incorporated company also provides tremendous tax advantages.

Here is why I make This Suggestion:

While it is true that other tax haven jurisdictions may be a better choice for general asset protection or tax strategies, any investor considering the Dominican Republic should form a separate Dominican Company for the following reasons:

1. Title of Real Estate and Bank Accounts

The Dominican Republic is an emerging market. With less than 16% of the tourists coming from the US, it has also remained sort of an undiscovered market for many investors. Because of this, The Dominican Republic offers some of the best real estate bargains and returns from time deposit investments in the entire Caribbean, but obscurity has its price. The meaning is that The Dominican Republic is not as sophisticated as say the Bahamas or Panama with regards to foreign ownership of real estate or investments. While the new legislation has greatly liberalized and improved foreign ownership of land, most government offices and banks are not familiar with the idea of property that is being purchased or titled in the name of an offshore trust or IBC. You will have a difficult time getting property or bank accounts titled in the name of a US Delaware corporation, Bahamas IBC or other offshore entity. Not because it is against the law or because of some other issue, simply because Dominicans are not used to dealing with these type of structures and do not have the experience. So, to have an asset protection program in place for your Dominican holdings and to prevent a slew of tap dancing at the title transfer office (or down at the bank), the formation of local company speeds things up and prevents questions. Also, generally speaking, it is always a good idea to compartmentalize your holdings anyway. The meaning is, keep your investments or properties separated.

2. The New Capital Gains Tax

The real benefit to owning your Vacation Property or other real estate through a local Dominican Corporation is tax savings. Most foreign investors are unaware of the very recent capital gains tax imposed into the tax code. The fact of the matter is, I would wager to guess that most Dominicans are probably not aware of it either. If you ask most Dominican Real Estate agents, they will most likely give you the boiler plate reply regarding title transfer tax, but may indicate that there is no capital gains tax in the Dominican Republic. While this used to be true in the past, it is not the case today. Fear not, there is a solution.

Most governments assess capital gains and property title transfer taxes when a property title changes hands. This is true for real estate in the United States, Europe or Tim-bok-tu. The solution then is to never change the title of ownership. If the property title name does not change, there is no title transfer tax, nor is there an official sales document indicating the new purchase price (and thus a way to determine the capital gain due). Instead, sell or transfer the entity that owns the real estate through a private transaction. Not only is this perfectly legal, it is also a common practice that wealthy Dominicans have been doing for years.

In reality, the new buyer is not taking direct possession of the property; they are taking control, via stock ownership and/or the directorship, of a company that happens to own the property. Thus eliminating a taxable real estate transaction.

How to Form a Dominican Company

Articles of Incorporation - Like most jurisdictions, a standard document is drafted to indicate the company purpose, tenants, direction and officers. The company purpose can be as general or as specific as the client wishes. We suggest, as with all of our client incorporations, that the articles include such language that gives the client complete and sole authority over bank accounts or company contracts.

Company Name - Since most foreigners are not aware of the Dominican Incorporation, you will not find many companies in the registrar that contain names in other than the Spanish Language.

I've seen, however, successfully incorporated company names in the English language for clients. All Dominican companies end with the denotation of C x A or S.A. The C x A notation is uniquely used in the Dominican Republic, but just like the terms "Inc, Ltd. or S.A.", indicates that this is an incorporated company. As with other jurisdictions, clients must provide three choices of the company name to make sure that the desired name is not currently registered or in use by another incorporated company.

Authorized Capital - The authorized capital of the company must be expressed in Dominican Pesos and can be any amount the client wishes. For the purpose of initial costs, taxes and the annual registration fee, we suggest that the client form the company with the minimum required capital, which is 10,000 Dominican Pesos or less than US$800 under current exchange rates. The authorized capital is indicated on the incorporation documents, but the client need not prove this amount via bank deposit or otherwise.

Stockholders or Founders - Unlike some jurisdictions, the Dominican company does require that seven individuals form the company. Usually, these persons are also the stockholders as well, but certainly do not necessarily have control. This is accomplished for the client through the use of six nominee Dominican shareholders, with the client either acting the first dominant shareholder with 94% of the stock, or by the client's other offshore entity as the predominant shareholder.

Directors of the Company - The Dominican Company requires that three individuals are assigned to take the positions of President, Vice-President and Secretary. Usually it is suggested that the client take the position of President, and as such is the only director who is duly authorized to sign on bank accounts or engage in other business on behalf of the company. We also suggest that a spouse or other trusted person be named as the Secretary for convenience of authorizing company resolutions (see the company seal or "Sello")

.

Company Seal or "Sello" - Each Dominican company must use a company seal, which only the secretary will use in conjunction with his or her signature to verify company documents or resolutions.

Tax Liabilities of the Company - Your Dominican company enjoys the benefit of tax free bank account or time deposit interest. Assuming the company is not engaged in any local commerce, no tax liabilities will be due other than the minimal annual registration tax, which is currently less than US$850 based upon the 10,000 peso authorized share capital and related annual maintenance fees. If clients intend to rent out their property that is owned by the Dominican company, clients are advised to speak with a professional, regarding strategies to eliminate a local taxable income possibility. A local accountant will be required to complete an annual tax statement or "Declaration de Renta" indicating that the company had no taxable income for the previous year. This can be easily accomplished and costs less than US$200 for this service

Chapter 9

Obtaining Residency in the Dominican Republic

The Process for Obtaining Residency and a Second Passport

Dominican residency is a very useful status to acquire for a variety of reasons:

1) It facilitates a number of business transactions in the D.R., including obtaining bank loans, buying real estate and applying for credit; 2) It makes one eligible for lower tuition at Dominican universities; 3) It permits one to work legally in the Dominican Republic; 4) One can take advantage of Law 14-93, Art. 13, and import most household goods duty free.

In order to obtain Dominican residency, it is first necessary to obtain a residence visa. Even if one is already in the Dominican Republic under another kind of visa, such as a tourist card or tourist visa or business visa, a residence visa must be applied for and obtained before obtaining a provisional residence card, which is the final document certifying that one has valid Dominican residency. While in practice it is not necessary to be a legal resident to live in the Dominican Republic, the principal advantage is that you will be able to import your household goods, most tax exempt, under Law 14-93.

Residence Visa

In order to obtain a residency visa, a number of documents must be submitted to the Dominican consulate nearest the actual place of residency of the applicant, or if the applicant is already in the Dominican Republic, they may be submitted to the Secretary of State for Foreign Relations of the Dominican Republic. The documents are the following:

- ✓ Three 2" x 2" frontal photos of the applicant's face.
- ✓ A completed Visa application Form 509.
- ✓ A certification of good behavior issued by the Police Department of the applicant's original place of residence.
- ✓ An employment agreement or, if a real estate investment has been made, a copy of the purchase agreement, or any other documentation proving the applicant's financial solvency in the Dominican Republic. The employment agreement must be registered with the Dominican Secretariat of Labor which will send a labor inspector to the place of work to determine work conditions and ensure that the foreign applicant is filling a position that a Dominican national cannot at the moment fill. The process of certifying the employment agreement is separate from that of applying for residency, and may take some time, in most cases, up to one month after filing the agreement with the Labor Department before one can proceed to file any documentation with the Ministry of Foreign Relations.
- ✓ A letter of guarantee from a Dominican citizen, or legal resident of the Dominican Republic.
- ✓ If a real estate investment has been made, a copy of the Presidential authorization if one had been obtained.
- ✓ The results of a medical examination certified by a Notary Public and authenticated by the Dominican consul.
- ✓ An original birth certificate of the applicant, translated into Spanish.

Once the above documents are assembled, the file is complete and may be submitted to the Consular Section of the Ministry of Foreign Affairs on Avenida Independencia, some 300 meters east of the Santo Domingo Hotel. The Ministry of Foreign Affairs is housed in a former residence of Rafael Leonidas Trujillo, the former dictator.

The file eventually will be sent to the Intelligence Service of the Dominican Republic known by its acronym in Spanish, DNI. This department will schedule an interview with the applicant and his guarantor to determine the validity of the application. This is normally a routine matter which is to confirm the information already provided by the client to the government. Once this is done the file is then returned to the Secretary of Foreign Affairs for further processing.

The entire process for obtaining the residence visa may take between two to three months, although some cases have been known to take as much as one year.

Provisional Residence Card

After the residence visa has been issued, the applicant has 60 days within which to enter the Dominican Republic, or if already here, 60 days within which to submit an application for a provisional residence card. This application is submitted to the Dominican Immigration Department which normally takes some two to three months to process. It is valid for one year at the end of which time the applicant may submit a petition for a permanent residence card. Permanent residence cards must be renewed every year. If five years elapse after a permanent residence card has expired, the applicant loses his residency.

The requirements for applying for a provisional residence card are the following:

- ✓ Application Form C-1 Ref.

- ✓ Two copies of the Residence Visa.

- ✓ A copy of the applicant's birth certificate, translated into Spanish.

- ✓ Four 2" x 2" frontal photos of the applicant's face.

- ✓ Three 2" x 2" profile photos of the applicant's face.

- ✓ A copy of the land purchase agreement, Certificate of Title issued by the Title Registry office or a copy of the employment agreement or other documentation proving the financial solvency of the applicant in the Dominican Republic.

127

✓ A notarized letter from a Dominican citizen or a legal resident in the country, guaranteeing the Dominican government the financial support of the applicant during his or her stay in the country, including, if need be, the cost of repatriating the applicant.

✓ The results of a physical examination, including a blood test (V.D.R.L.), an HIV test and a chest x-ray, conducted by a medical doctor who is a citizen of the Dominican Republic.

✓ Immigration Department excise taxes.

Permanent Residence Card

Once the provisional residence card has expired, the applicant may then apply for a permanent residence card. The following documents are required in order to apply for the permanent residency card:

✓ Sworn statement by two persons who bear witness to knowing the applicant in the country and that his conduct is in compliance with the laws of the country (plus three copies).
✓ Letter of guarantee notarized by a local attorney to the effect that a Dominican citizen or resident will assume responsibility for the applicant while in the country (plus three copies).
✓ Four copies of the residence visa issued by the Secretariat of Foreign Affairs for the provisional residency.
✓ The original provisional residency card plus three copies.
✓ A certificate of good conduct issued by the Dominican police plus three copies.
✓ Six 2" x 2" photos, four of them frontal photos and two profile photos of the applicant.
✓ The results of a physical examination, including a blood test (V.D.R.L.), an HIV test and a chest x-ray, conducted by a medical doctor who is a citizen of the Dominican Republic.
✓ Bank letter certifying to an applicant's accounts in a Dominican bank.

✓ Copy of an employment agreement, if an applicant is working in the Dominican Republic.
✓ Application Form C-1 duly completed.

Chapter 10

Managing Your Rental Property

Now you have located a property, put an offer in, had your offer accepted, went through the closing procedure, and secured proper title to your investment. Now the fun begins!

If your plans are to only use your property for personal use, than only a small portion of this chapter will pertain to you. Although it is quite possible at this point to leave your property alone until the time comes when you will visit the Dominican Republic, I highly advise finding some local help in managing the property. By managing the property in this sense, I mean finding landscapers, pool cleaners, security guards, and people to help with the general up keep of the property.

If you purchased a condo, or raw land, the property will be basically maintenance free. But if you purchased a villa you will need to do some searching. For the owners not interested in renting the property out, I would advise a trip to the Dominican in which you will search out and secure at the very least, a landscaping company. These companies can be found throughout all areas of the country and are essential in keeping up the appearance of the property.

Keeping up the appearance of the property will benefit you in more than just aesthetics. By having a property that is up kept it will appear that the property is being lived in and will help deter possible vandalism and theft. Ideally, hiring a security guard would be the best protection, but sometimes that is not financially reasonable.

So where do you start?

Now that you've closed on your Caribbean Paradise it is time get moving. For the time being we are going to be speaking about condos and villas. Land purchases are a whole different animal and isn't really relevant to this next section.

What I recommend doing after closing is planning on spending at least one full week in the Dominican. If you can swing more time, more is better in this case. This week will not be a relaxing week in the sun. There will be plenty of time for those kinds of weeks in the future. This week will be to get you situated in your new condo or villa.

This week your goals should be to:

1. Clean and prepare the place for vacationing.
2. Furnish the place (if you weren't lucky enough to buy it pre furnished)
3. Find suitable management (if you plan on using a company rather than do it by owner)
4. Take care of all the luxuries that you will need to accommodate the people staying in the condo villa (things like internet, cable…)

In this chapter I am going to help you set your goals for this week, create a check list of tasks to perform, and use your time as wisely as possible.

First Week of Ownership Checklist

✓ If renting: Contact several management companies to discuss options and fees
✓ For Villa owners: Contact landscaping companies for fees and options
✓ Purchase necessary furnishings for villa or condo
✓ If renting: Get villa in suitable renting condition
✓ If renting: Take as many flattering pictures of place as possible
✓ Contact phone, internet, cable, and utility companies
✓ Meet and greet neighbors

As you can see, the first item on the list is for owners looking to rent out their property. While I will go into much more detail about the pros and cons of a management company in a later section, I think every owner should take the time to see for themselves what these companies offer and what kind of fees they charge. These are people who specialize in renting condos/villas to foreign travelers. At the very least you will gain some knowledge and insight from this meeting. Even if you eventually decide not to use the service of a management company, the short time you spend speaking with them can be invaluable in terms of practical advice you might acquire.

These companies are not difficult to find. I recommend going online and setting up the meeting before you leave for the DR. That way while you are down there you are not burdened with wasting time looking for a company. Your meeting will already be set up and you can concentrate on your other list items. If you do find that you are having a difficult time locating a management company, I suggest speaking with local real estate brokers and see who they usually recommend to their clients. The agent (assuming you used a broker for your purchase) will probably have a company that he or she recommends. That is a good starting point, but I always recommend talking to several companies.

During your meeting with the management company it is important that you pick their brains for as much knowledge as you can get. They are the best source of information on the quickest way to complete the other items on your checklist. They will surely know of landscaping companies, utilities services, and cable/internet providers. Take notes during this meeting and you should be able to gather enough information from this meeting that the rest of your list is a breeze.

If you are unable to get landscapers phone numbers from the management company you meet with, there are several other ways you can go about getting this information. One of the best ways is to talk with the neighbors. All of your neighbors have a company that they use for these services. Chances are most of them are using the same company. Find out what that company is and contact them. This is a good company to start with as you can be sure that they are a legitimate operating company, and your neighbors serve as references you can judge their performance by.

If it is at all possible I always recommend buying previously furnished apartments, condos, or villas. They might cost a little bit more but it will save you a lot of time and aggravation in the long run.

Furnishing your place is only as difficult as you make it. If you have a clear idea of how you want to decorate the place, the best idea might be to bring as much as possible from your home country when you take your first journey down there. Most airlines only allow a certain amount of luggage on the plane per passenger, so check with your carrier to see what your limits are.

Once you get down there your shopping choices will be limited. Unless you are buying your condo or villa in Santo Domingo or Santiago you will probably have to travel to find specific items that you are looking for. If it is possible to take a road trip to either of these cities that may be your best bet. They will offer the best selection of all goods. In the beach towns you will be able to buy basic furnishings and amenities, but your choice in quality and design will be limited to a few stores. The bigger cities such as Santo Domingo and Santiago will give you a wider selection to choose from.

If your place does not come pre-furnished here is a short list of some essential things you will need to begin with:

- Blankets
- Mattress pads
- Phones
- Lamps
- TV
- Stereo
- DVD
- Pillow cases
- Garbage cans
- Alarm clocks
- Vacuum cleaner
- Pillows
- Iron and ironing board
- Shower liner
- Plungers
- Couches/chairs/tables
- Silverware
- Glasses/cups/bowls/plates

- Pots and pans
- Refrigerator
- Cleaning supplies

Just to give you an idea of some things you might want to consider adding to your place but are not necessities:

- Doors mats
- Beach chairs/umbrella
- Patio set
- Board games
- BBQ grill and utensils
- Hot tub
- Bikes
- Safety boxes
- Hair dryer
- First aid kit
- Pictures
- Coffee pot
- Microwave
- Tupperware

I'm sure there are plenty of other items that you will add to your list of things you'll need for your new place. The key is not to overwhelm one self. Get the essential items first and slowly begin to acquire the rest of your list over time. If you plan on renting the place out you will need to acquire these things faster. In a later section I will list additional things you might want to furnish your place with to leave your guests more satisfied and more likely to recommend your place out or rent again in the future.

Getting your Condo/Villa in suitable renting condition

Whether or not you plan on renting out your investment property you will want to do a thorough cleaning. If you are purchasing a newly built and empty place this is not as important as if you are purchasing a previously lived in condo, apartment, or villa.

Many of the condo complexes charge monthly fees to the owners. These fees usually include maid service. This is only true of the bigger complexes. If you purchase a condo that includes maid service then that is one less thing that you have to worry about. If your condo doesn't include maid service I would do a good deep cleaning while you are down there that week. In most cases I would usually recommend hiring a service or cleaning lady to perform the work, so that you can spend your time performing other tasks, but some people like the excitement of getting a new place in shape.

Getting your place in shape includes doing a complete cleaning job. This means getting rid of all garbage and waste that has accumulated in your vacation home. It is also a smart idea to set some bug and ant killers throughout the place. There are many areas of the Dominican that have quite the bug problem. If the place hasn't been lived in for awhile there may be a huge infestation of insects. You can call a local exterminator or you can purchase some "bombs" yourself and set them off when you will be away from the place for a few hours or even over night.

If you plan on renting out your property and you don't belong to a condo association that is equipped with a cleaning service now is a good time to contact different services and request information about rates and options. Finding a cleaning service will not be a difficult task. If you plan on hiring a management company they will most likely take care of this for you, but you will pay a premium for every service a management company offers. In a later section I will go over the pros and cons of going with one of these services. If you need help locating a cleaning service I would approach this the same way that I recommended you approach finding a landscaping service. You can ask your neighbors, ask local realtors, or simply drive around and look for signs. In a relatively poor country like the Dominican there is no shortage of people looking for work.

Taking Pictures (for renters)

For those of you who have decided that you are going to take the course of renting out your property I am going to give you an important piece of information: Take as many high quality pictures of your property as possible.

In all likelihood your main source of leads for the rental of your property will come from various websites. Remember, these websites lists hundreds of places, so if you want your property to stand out over all the others you will desperately need some good photographs.

Think about how you make your decision when looking through brochures on hotels to stay out. Most likely you choose the hotel that looks the best in the pictures. You probably know from experience that pictures can be deceiving. But that is beyond the point. The point is to make these pictures get as much mileage as possible.

Do not cheap out on the pictures. Do not take the pictures with a Polaroid, or a disposal camera. The quality of the pictures will make a big difference in how they appear on the various websites. If you don't already own a digital camera I would recommend going out and purchasing one. You can get a decent mid range one for around $200. I would go to a shop that specializes in them and explain to the salesperson what your needs are. They will help you choose a camera that will take the best pictures. More than likely you will want a camera that has a fish eye lens. This will enable you to take broader shots of the rooms.

I would wait until you have cleaned the place up and furnished it a bit to take the pictures. Here are some helpful hints for taking pictures.
- Take as many pictures of the pool as you can. Try different angles to see which one portrays it the best. The pool is often a huge selling point to people considering renting.
- Take as many flattering pictures of the kitchen as possible. Women love a nice kitchen. If you can get some good shots of the kitchen they will be worth their weight in gold.
- If you are close to the beach, take shots of the ocean. Take pictures of the local scenery.
- Take some pictures of near by bars and restaurants and attractions. Many of the possible renters will have never been to the Dominican so they will be interested to see what kind of area your place resides in.

- Take several pictures of each room from all different angles. The goal is to take as many pictures as it takes to narrow it down to 10 or so really good ones. All the bad ones will be deleted.
- If you have a ladder-use it. If you don't have a ladder, stand on a chair. You will be able to get views from higher and up and give a different feel to the room.
- Stage the pictures to capture the essence of the place. Make use of candles, pillows, fireplaces, balconies, and the like.
- When taking pictures of the bedroom be sure to dress the bed up as nice as possible. Many couples renting will be interested in seeing what kind of sleeping arrangements they will have.
- Make the living room look as cozy as possible. If you have plants, pictures, coffee tables, board games, display these items to give the place a homely feel.
- Make sure not to clutter the bathroom before taking photographs. Unlike the other rooms, less is more, should be your philosophy for the bathroom.
- If you have a hot tub or deck or sauna set the stage for these pictures. Don't have anyone it them, but leave wine glasses, towels, beach balls, hard cover novel for maximum romantic appeal.
- Set the table. Use attractive silverware if possible.

Contact Utility Companies and set up Phone, Internet, and Cable, and Security

More than likely you are going to want some amenities to go along with your new purchase. These include services like cable tv, high speed internet, phone service, and security systems.

For the most part these services will cost you similar rates as you would pay in the United States. If you are purchasing a condo complex some of them will include wireless internet and cable TV. It is a good question to ask the seller. Purchasing a condo that includes internet and cable could save you $100 a month in fees. Most condo associations will handle your electric bill for you as well. This does not mean that they include the bill in your monthly dues. This just means that the association will take care of making sure there is electricity available. They will divide up the bills each month and send each owner their responsible share.

If you're condo or villa is not already equipped with cable, internet, or phone they are all fairly simple to set up. If you go into town there will be a good selection of stores that offer these services. You can shop around several stores and try to find the best rates.

DSL is also available through your cable TV service, though I have not tried it. I use Verizon, VIP Flash, and the total cost is about 80 bucks a month, with a few long distance calls thrown in. DSL is not cheap either.

An option that some people use for phone service is Skype. This is basically a phone service that will be through your computer. This is good for those who will be making lots of overseas calls while spending time in the Dominican Republic. Skype is extremely easy to set up, and only requires an internet connection and a headset.

Check out www.skype.com for more details.

Although the Dominican Republic is a safer country by most standards I still would recommend installing a security system. If you will not be living there full time, this means that much of the time the place will be vacant. A vacant property is an invitation to thieves and vandalisms. Security systems are not that expensive and can be installed rather quickly while you are down there.

Check out http://www.issltt.com/site/index.php for some of your options.

Meet and Greet Neighbors

One thing I always advise new owners of real estate in the Dominican to do is greet the neighbors. I recommend this for a variety of reasons:

1. These people will be able to recommend reliable management companies, cable companies, utilities, phone, landscapers, maids, pool cleaners, security guards, and so on. They have experience dealing with

138

the very people you are looking to hire. I'm sure if asked they will be willing to share some information.

2. They will know the best local places to go for food, furniture, supplies, and so on.
3. The friendlier you are with them the more likely they'll be to watch your place when you're not around.
4. There are times you might need a favor from one of these people in the future. It is a lot easier to ask for a favor if you've previously introduced yourself.
5. If you plan on spending a lot of time at your new property it is always nice to make friends with the neighbors. These are people you can socialize with.

It won't always be possible to meet the neighbors. Many of your neighbors may not be living in the Dominican full time. Some of them will have rented the condo or villa out and the people living there now are only short term renters. Do not let this discourage you. The more people you talk to the more likely you are to be sent the way of someone who can be of true help to you.

If you are uncomfortable just knocking on doors, another option for you is to ask your broker to introduce you to some other foreigners who've made the Dominican their home. This will take the pressure off you, and your broker is usually more than happy to help as it increases his chance of a referral in the future.

To Hire a Management Company or To Rent by Owner

One of the more difficult decisions that a new vacation home owner is faced with is whether or not to employ the services of a management company. In the last section I advised you to go and talk with a management company merely to pick their brains about all things related to your new home. This meeting will give you a chance to feel out what these companies have to offer. In this section I will give you the pros and cons of hiring a company or renting by owner.

Using a Management Company

The strongest argument for the use of a management company is convenience. There is a relaxed confidence that most owners feel knowing that the responsibility of renting and managing their property is in the hands of competent professionals. For some there is no price tag for this pleasure.

Owning a property a few thousand miles from your home can be quite intimidating. The thought of trying to manage that particular property from your home base can be downright paralyzing with fear. Are all the fears warranted? No. Is there potential for major headaches when declining to use a professional service? Yes. But there is a risk reward factor that we will discuss later in this chapter.

Most real estate brokers act as property managers. So as you can see by the amount of brokers flooding the Dominican Republic, there is no shortage of management companies. But like choosing any professional service, there will be good companies and there will be bad companies.

A good management company's job is to get your place rented as much as possible, for as much money as possible, and to maintain your property while you are away. The responsibilities of these companies include but are not limited to:

- Placing ads for your property on the internet and sometimes in local newspapers.
- Screening prospective renters and collecting all deposits and payments.
- Making the sure the place is continually in renting condition.
- Sometimes meeting and greeting guests at airport
- Dealing with possible problems at the property such as plumbing, security issues
- Doing general maintenance on the property
- Keeping records of all rental transactions

Here are some more specifics functions that some management companies will provide its clients:

- Personnel Management – recruit, train, manage, terminate and financially liquidate employees.

- Payroll Tax Payments & Compliance – prepare and distribute payroll taxes based on the payroll for your property at the frequency necessary to meet Dominican Republic labor laws.
- Vehicle Maintenance & Insurance – provide periodic maintenance checkups and cleaning of your vehicle to keep it in top operating condition. Provide complete vehicle insurance program providing collision and liability coverage. Ensure registration and inspections are kept up to date and current.
- Property & Liability Insurance – recommend and offer complete insurance programs and umbrella liability policies for your property.
- Grounds & Facilities Maintenance – oversight of your private property maintenance to ensure gardens, walls, fences, beach, beach access, generators and the like are properly maintained, including fuel consumption monitoring, noise abatement recommendations and so forth.
- Primary Local Contact – act as your local contact for vendors, service providers, employees and others requiring a local decision maker here in the Dominican Republic.

Here is a list of some of the extra services that some companies offer at additional costs:

- Arrange airport collection and drop off
- Arrange introduction pack for property
- Secure a car and driver if required
- Full personal amber care
- Local orientations
- Babysitting services
- Laundry services
- DVD and Video rentals
- Grocery shopping

As you can see property management companies can offer much more than simply listing your property on a website and collecting rents. Like I said earlier, their job is basically to make you and your renter's lives as convenient and comfortable as possible.

Draw backs of a management company

This is not saying there are no downsides to hiring a property management company. For every good story you hear about management companies you will hear an equally bad story from an upset owner.

One of the biggest things detracting a property owner from hiring a property manager is the cost associated with it. Generally a property manager will take between 15-30% of the rental fee. This fee only constitutes the basic services such as advertising the property, collecting rents, overseeing maintenance, cleaning after each rental, and being on call for possible problems.

Resolving these "possible problems" are all additional costs. For instance, if there is a plumbing problem requiring the services of a professional, the management company will hire the professional and send you the bill. In addition to the professionals invoice the management company will generally tack on 10% or more as their fee. This is one reason that hiring a reputable management company is a must. There are a lot of people out there that prey on naiveté's of some foreigners and will take them for a financial roller coaster of a ride sucking them for every penny they can get.

Another reason that hiring a property manager to rent out your property is sometimes less than advantageous, is that you lose control over who rents out your home. Property managers make their money by renting your home as often as possible. Because of this fact they are not as selective about whom they will rent your property to.

For instance, a friend of mine who owns a condo in Cabarete has a management company that does his renting for him. His condo has three bedrooms and can ideally sleep 6-8 people max. My friend has maintenance guy that does some work periodically on his condo. The maintenance guy informed in one weekend that there were at least 12 college students staying in his condo. The management company is not going to turn down a rental, but had my friend been self-managing he never would have allowed 12 people to sleep in his three bedroom place.

I am not going to stereotype college students, but I used to be one of them and I feel bad for the folks who rented me their ski houses and beach houses back then. While this is not true of all college students, the vast majority of large groups of students are on vacation to party hard. There is nothing wrong with hard partying if it doesn't involve things in your home get broken. There is just too much room for error when there are massive amounts of partying involved. Things will break, doors will be left unlocked, there is potential for even bigger disasters like fires or injury.

The other disadvantage of having a management company do your renting for you is that you lack that rapport with the renters. If you are self-managing your home then you will most likely be the one who handles the rental inquires and takes the deposits and so forth. This time dealing with the renter allows you to build some rapport with them. The more rapport you build with them the more likely they will be to take better care of the place. If you can come across friendly and sincere they will most likely respond with a friendly and sincere approach to staying in your home.

Another disadvantage of using a property management company is that you lack control of the vacancies. Property managers do not always have your best interests in mind. Many times these companies will have hundreds of customers to worry about. They have to appease many people. How does this affect you? Management companies will sometimes sell a mid-week rental leaving valuable, easy to rent days open. What the company is doing is taking the easy way out. But the easy way is not always the best way for you. A management companies looks at it this way: the company may have 100 rental homes that it manages. What does the company do if it gets 100 qualified renters? Does the company try to match the renter's needs to the right properties for the right dates, regardless of which properties get the most booking? The answer is no. If the company did that then certain units would out rent other units and the company would have hear complaints from various owners as to why certain units were being rented more than other units. Because of this the management company spreads the qualified renters around. The company will try to make sure that each owner gets one week booked. It's all about semi appeasing many people rather than doing a terrific job for a few people.

Like I said earlier though, the biggest thing keeping people from using the services of a management company is money. If you take a look at our break even formula using a management company you will see what I mean. Let's say you rent 12 peak weeks and 5 other weeks. For every week you rent, management companies take an average of 30% for commissions. So if you were getting $2000 in rent it now becomes $1400. The management company is likely to add on other costs before the weeks are over. What this means is that you will wind up having to rent the place 27 weeks instead of 17 weeks to net the same amount of cash in your pocket. With a management company you will need to rent 10 more weeks to come up with the same money. You have to ask yourself is convenience worth the price?

The Pros and Cons of Self Management

Money

Obviously the biggest advantage of renting by owner is money. You will see more of the money that comes in from your rentals if you're not forking over 30% to a management company. Besides the rental fees you will save on the cleaning and maintenance fees as you won't have to pay the hefty surcharge these companies add to providing these services.

Screening

Renting by owner is also beneficial in the fact that it gives you complete control over whom you rent to. As we mentioned earlier giving management companies complete control over who rents your property means that at some point you are likely to get undesirable tenants. These are tenants who will not have regards to your personal property and not treat the house or condo with the respect you wish. Although this can not be entirely avoided by renting by owner it can be reduced. This is because renting by owner allows you to personally scream all potential tenants.

You can speak with them and ask them any question that you like. If you decide that it is not in your best interest to rent to them, you don't have to. Also, people tend to take better care of the rented property when they have a little rapport with the owner. They will be more likely to treat the home as if it was their own if they get to know you over the phone or email a bit. When it's strictly business as usual with management companies many tenants forget that a human being actually owns the house and not some big bad corporation.

144

I find its most important to screen the possible tenants over the phone. This allows you the opportunity to convey the fact that you are a nice friendly person renting your home and not the big bad corporation that many people perceive. When you're speaking on the phone withhold whether or not the place is available. Always tell them that you think the place is available but you have to double check your date book. This gives you an out if you decide not to rent to them.

There are certain questions that you want to ask all potential renters. One of the first questions to ask is how many adults and how many children will be staying in your property. This allows you to see if your property will even suit their needs. If your property is clearly too small for them there is no reason to be dishonest and tell them they'll all fit. An unhappy tenant is helpful to no one. It also allows you the opportunity to screen out large groups of young adults who might be looking to use your property as a frat house for the week. I lived in a frat house, so trust me you don't want your vacation home looking like one. You can easily access this information by simply asking the age of the parties involved. Most of the time they'll tell you without thinking twice. At this point if you decide you'd rather not rent to them you just use your out and tell them "sorry but I just checked and the property was actually rented." There will be no hard feelings that way and you can find a more suitable tenant for that week, and they are free to find a more suitable frat house.

Beware of Scams

Also remember when screening possible renters to beware of scammers. The internet is filled with people looking to take advantage of the unsuspecting. One of the biggest scams to be aware of is the "Cashier check." This scam involves a renter paying you with a cashier's check that is in excess of the actual rent. The renter sends you the cashier's check which looks completely legit, and will be initially accepted at most banks. While you're waiting for the check to clear, the renter will cancel his trip and ask for his deposit back. You will send him his deposit back, only to later find that the check did not clear and was counterfeit.

Most of the time these scammers will contact you by email. Usually they will have a story that involves a third party paying for them with a cashier's check. I find that if the email seems suspect ask for a credit card to hold the deposit on.

Most law abiding citizens have at least one credit card they can give you. As a rule I would say don't accept cashier's checks. It is not worth the risk. Most people around the world are able to pay with credit cards, personal checks, or pay pal. I highly recommend only accepting those methods of payment. Never agree to accept more than the amount due. And never send money back for over payment.

Vacancies

If you decide to manage the property yourself you will have better control over when the property is rented. Management companies serve many different owners and have to appease all of them. While at times this is to your benefit, at other times it is a hindrance to you. An example of this is a management company selling a midweek rental leaving very valuable, easy to rent days open. Remember these companies are most likely spreading their pool of renters between the fifty to hundred properties they manage. This means that they are not necessarily connecting renters with the best property (which could be yours) so much as they are evening up the booking between owners.

Personal Use

Another benefit of self management is the fact that you will have more control over when you and your friends and family can make use of your property. Just recently a friend of mine who owns in Cabarete was complaining because his management company rented out his condo for the same week that he promised his parents that they could use it. He says he left a note with the company but they went ahead and booked it anyway claiming they never received the email. This is an example of what can happen when you put other people in charge of renting out your property. You tend to lose a little bit of control over the property. Some management companies will go as far as to tell owners that they won't allow them to occupy the property during the peek weeks such as the week of Christmas. This is because the management company doesn't want to lose their cut of guaranteed peak rental rates.

Cash Flow

Like I said earlier though, the biggest thing keeping people from using the services of a management company is money. If you take a look at our break even formula using a management company you will see what I mean. Let's say you rent 12 peak weeks and 5 other weeks. For every week you rent, management companies take an average of 30% for commissions. So if you were getting $2000 in rent it now becomes $1400. The management company is likely to add on other costs before the weeks are over. What this means is that you will wind up having to rent the place 27 weeks instead of 17 weeks to net the same amount of cash in your pocket. With a management company you will need to rent 10 more weeks to come up with the same money. You have to ask yourself is convenience worth the price? Self management will put more money in your pocket. Below is the flip side to that as I list the draw backs of self management.

Draw backs of Self Management

Managing your rental property yourself will take time out of your day. If you're the kind of person who likes to make an investment, sit back, and forget about it other than collecting checks every month then self management is not for you. If you are managing yourself there are certain responsibilities you will have to take care on a weekly or monthly basis. Here is a list of things you will need to do:

- Make sure your property is continually being advertised for rent
- Answer phone and email inquiries about your property
- Collect deposits and rental checks from potential renters
- Arrange for daily, weekly, and monthly maintenance of property
- Arrange cleaning after every renter leaves
- Be a problem solver in the event of a customer complaint

What scares most people away from self management is the last one on the list. Most people fear having to solve problems in a destination so far away. The reality is that most things can be handled with ease from the comfort of a computer. As long as you have a list of emergency contacts in the Dominican Republic you will be alright. Your list should include doctors, plumbers, electricians, local authorities, cleaning services, and lock smiths. It is rare that you will need to contact these people but if you have them in your rolodex it will make the times you do need to contact them a lot easier.

Another drawback is that some people are simply not good at keeping accurate records. A big part of management is customer relations, planning, and record keeping. This is important so that you don't over book a week, you are on top of collecting money due, you are aware of your monthly expenses, and your bills are paid on time. Some people are just too busy to take care of these things on their own, and others just aren't cut out to be managers. If you fit into one of these two categories than it might be wise for you to sacrifice a little of your cash flow for the peace of mind of knowing things are running smoothly. (This is assuming you've hired a competent, trust worthy Management Company)

Chapter Review

The decision of whether or not to hire a management company is not one that you have to make immediately. If you decide to rent your property you can do so without the services of a management company for a trial period. During this trial period you can evaluate the time you will need to dedicate to performing the tasks needed to properly manage the property. If after the trial period you decide that you can handle the work than you can decline to hire the services of the company. If on the other hand, you feel over whelmed by the responsibilities that go along with self management than you should consider hiring one of the companies.

In the next chapter I am going to discuss your options for marketing the property if you decide to rent by owner.

Chapter 11

Marketing Your Rental Property

The single most important element that will determine whether or not you will make money renting your vacation home is your ability to successfully market it. Sure without marketing your property you will still have the occasional friends and family renting your place, but you will be missing out on a huge pool of potential renters that are willing to pay a premium for your place.

A good competent management company will market your property in the manner that they market all of their other properties. This manner may work for them, but is also may be limiting the amount of rentals you have the potential to receive. Most of these rental companies will promote a few properties on various websites with the hope of drawing renters in with the bait and switch. This is a time tested real estate marketing strategy that works extremely well for the brokers. But it does not always work extremely well for the owners whose properties are being managed. Remember, a management company's primary interest is making themselves money. This is why I recommend taking an active role in marketing your property whether you have hired the services of a management company or not.

Some management companies want full control of the marketing of the property. They only want the property marketed on their sites. I don't agree with this concept and would recommend not listing your property with a company that follows this policy. I usually like to work with companies that will allow you to find your own renters, and in turn they take little or no commission for the renters they did not supply. This allows you to be marketing the property as well. The key to a relationship like this is communication. You need to be constantly updating each other about what dates are available. It is easy to double book a week if you are not paying close attention to each other's rental activity.

Once you've established a rental policy you can begin your quest for effective, powerful advertising campaign. As I said earlier, it is advertising that will make or break you. In this chapter I am going to talk about ways that you can personally market your property.

Internet Marketing

In this day and age the most powerful tool in marketing your vacation home is the internet. The internet is extremely effective for marketing your property as well as communicating with the potential renters. The other beauty of the internet is that the cost involved is much lower than any other medium for advertising out there.

There are three different types of websites that you want to take into consideration when deciding how you are going to market your site online. In this chapter I will list some of the best sites out there. In the index of this book I include an even more comprehensive list of sites available for marketing your property. The three different types of sites that you should be taking advantage of are portal sites, personal site, and specialty sites.

Portal Sites

I discovered portal sites years ago while I was looking for an apartment to rent in Rio de Janeiro for a week. After putting a bunch of different key words into various search engines and finding different results I realized that most of the listings I was finding were all located on the same few sites. These sites are portal sites. A portal site is basically a site designed to match as many possible renters with as many possible homes. While some of the sites are free, most of these sites charge the property owner a fee for listing the property on the site. Some of the sites are a onetime fee, others a yearly fee, and other charge on a monthly or bi monthly basis.

These sites will basically give you a form to fill out regarding the property. The form will list basic information about the property, your personal rental rules and rates, and any additional information you want to include. Normally these sites will allow you to upload several pictures to be displayed with the site. Some of the more expensive sites will allow you to include a virtual tour. These sites will often allow you to link back to a personal site of the property, or your management company's site.

The great thing about these sites is that because of the huge amount of content they provide they are usually highly ranked in the search engines. What this means is that people searching for "Dominican rental properties" have a good chance of being directed to one of these sites.

Portal sites are basically a giant classified section. Some of them will be specific to the Dominican Republic, most of the more successful ones cater to many different vacation destinations. These sites usually allow the user to continually narrow down their search until they find what they are looking for. An example would be a user going to the site and clicking a button titled rentals. This button will take them to a list of regions. On the list of regions the user would click Caribbean. This would then bring them to a list of Caribbean Islands. From this list the user would select the Dominican Republic. Some sights will narrow it down even further with a list of regions within the Dominican Republic. Most sights will allow the user to narrow down their search even further through categories like # of bedrooms, price range, availability, and property type.

When choosing a site to list with you want a site that is listed on the first page of all the major search engines like Google, Yahoo, MSN, AOL, and Ask. Remember the search results in the column on the right are paid ads so they are not necessarily the best possible results. In fact many of the ones on the right will be newcomers. I would recommend choosing one of the results that shows up without the help of ad money. But, like I said earlier I will give you a list later in this chapter of some good ones.

Most of these sites will give you the ability to easily create your listing with pictures, descriptions, and pricing information. You should also be able to easily log in and update any of the information that may need to change such as rates, photos, and availability. A good site will supply you with a calendar and reservation request form. Some of these sites have an accompanying newsletter that they will list your home in to be mailed to their subscriber list.

You should test the functionality of the sites as if you were a potential renter. This will give you an idea of how "user friendly" the site is. Here are some things that you should look out for:

- How easy is the site to navigate?
- Does the site allow you to do more specific searches?
- Can you search by available dates?
- Can you easily view availability through an online calendar?
- Does it have a help line for renters with questions?

The benefit of these portal sites is the vast audience that you will immediately be exposed to. But because you are one of many you will not have the opportunity to fully promote your home the way you many like. That is why I always recommend creating a personal page of your property and linking to that page from the portal site.

Here is a list of some of the best portal sites:

VRBO.com- this site charges a yearly fee of $179 to run your ad for the year. There are upgrades that you can opt for that will let you add more photos. This is one of my favorite sites to use when searching for a property to rent. The site has been around for awhile and it gets heavy traffic.

Escape Artist.com- This very popular site is among the least expensive at only $99 a year. The site also allows you up to 20 images. The only drawback of this site is that it is not exclusively a rental site, and can be a little difficult to navigate from the home page.

VacationRentals.com- Another site that gets heavy traffic, and gives you a one year ad for $148. Their ad comes with eight photos and an availability calendar.

A1Vacations.com- This site has two options: 12 months with 4 photos for $148 or 12 months with 12 photos for $178.

Home Away.com- This $299 package gets you listed on 5 sites for 12 months with 12 photos. The sites that you get listed on are Home Away, Cyber Rentals, Great Rentals, and A1 Vacations

VacationRentals411.com- This site is free for you basic listing which includes 9 photos. There are upgrade packages available that let you add many more features.

Specialized Websites

While "portal" sites will get you the maximum amount of exposure to the largest group of potential renters, they can sometimes be flooded with properties which make it hard for your property to rise above the competition. One way to overcome this obstacle is to list your property on specialty sites. These are websites that cater to the needs of certain groups of people.

For instance, Cabarete, DR is a well known location for kite boarding. Kite boarders from all over the world visit Cabarete during the peak seasons. There are many websites out there that cater to this group of people. A smart idea is to list your property on these websites. Of course you will need to have a personal website to add your link to.

Another example of a specialty sites are websites that cater to vacation home owners that allow pets. Many owners do not allow pets which makes it relatively easy to rise above the competition if you do. The most known website for this kind of marketing is www.petfriendlytravel.com. This site connects pet owners with vacation home owners that will allow them to bring their pets on vacation with them.

Other examples of specialty sites are sites devoted to fishing, or water sports. If there is a niche interest in the area of Dominican Republic you own, find sites that cater to that niche and advertise there. Another example, though not for everyone, is the singles traveler sites. Dominican Republic is a popular destination for singles looking for rendezvous with the native men and women. There are plenty of sites out there that cater to this type of traveler. This might be someplace that you decide to think about.

Personal Website

Your personal site is the website that you have built and you are in charge of maintaining. Your reason for creating this site is so that you have a platform to give the most detailed information about your property. Unlike the specialty and portal sites you will not have limits imposed on how many pictures you can upload, how many words you can use to describe your property. Basically with your own personal site you can be as thorough and creative as you'd like in presenting your property to the public.

You will link to your personal website from all of the other forms of advertising that you are a part of. If you are listed on portal and specialty sites they will most likely allow you to link over to your site. If you run an ad in the classifieds list your personal website along with your phone number. The purpose of the personal site is not as a form of advertising, but as an accompaniment to your other forms of advertising. Your personal site should be used as a selling tool to help convince potential renters that you're place is superior to the others listed on the various portal and specialty sites. You do this by including details, photos, in-depth information regarding your property's unique features.

Don't worry about getting this site ranked high in search engines. It won't be. Don't be concerned with that. The portal and specialty sites that you are listing your site on get the traffic that will direct them to your property. It can be also used to email a potential renter who has additional questions. The goal of this site is to sell them on your property once you get them there.

Building your personal site

The first step is to purchase a domain name. Something that is specific your property would work best, but is not necessary. An example of a good domain name for a personal website would be something along the lines of www.bocachicadream.com It is catchy, easy to remember, and is descriptive of the place you're trying to rent. Another example would be www.drhotspot.com. It is not necessary to make the title any longer than that.

After you purchase your domain name you must find someone to build your site (assuming you're not a web developer.) You can hire a college student for a couple hundred dollars or you can hire a web design company. It really depends on how much you want to spend, and what kind of features you are looking for.

If you are interested in getting a quote for a website you can contact www.hudsonhorizons.com.

Examples of Personal Sites

http://cabareterentals.com/

What you will need for your websites

- **One-Line description** Most sites will want you to provide a short, one line description of the property. An example: "Charming 3BR Villa with Ocean View and Private beach." View writing this as you would write a headline for a classified ad.
- **More detailed description** After your headline you will need to write a second description. Try to write at least 3-4 paragraphs (depending on what sites allow) Writing more than that may lose the renters attention. Look at this at your chance to make the sales pitch.
- **Photos** You will want to post some attention grabbing photos. Many potential renters will make their decisions based solely on the pictures. In previous chapter I gave some instructions for taking photos. Go back and reread that section if necessary.
- **Local Attractions** You also want to include what is in the area. Many potential renters aren't familiar with the different parts of the Dominican Republic. This is your opportunity to sell them on your area. Include any attractions, and quote any magazine headlines about the area such as "voted Conde Nast 100 Best Beaches." If it's close to a golf course or Trumps Marina, these are things you should mention.
- **Calendar** Most of the portal sites will have a calendar available for your potential renters. It is up to you though to keep the calendar up to date. It is extremely important that you do so. The more up to date your calendar is the more bookings you will receive. Vacation renters want the least amount of work possible to find the best place. Not having a calendar means they will have to email or call about availability. Most will not bother. If your calendar is not updated and has no booked dates they will assume something is wrong with the place.
- **Testimonials** Add some nice comments from previous renters. Once you've rented the place a few times you can ask the renters to leave some feedback. If they enjoyed your place they will do so gladly. Some portal sites will have a place for renters to leave reviews on your property.

Chapter 12

The Renter's FAQ

In this next chapter I will answer some of the most common questions that I have received over the years regarding renting property in the Dominican Republic. While it would be unrealistic of me to say that I will touch upon every question you might have, I will do my best to address as many potential questions as possible.

1. **Q:** *How do I know what to charge for my property?*

    A: To get the right price you will have to do research on other properties in the area and find out what they are charging. The best way to do this is act as if you were looking to rent a property in the Dominican Republic. Go on the internet and shop around. You can also call management companies in the area and see what similar properties are renting for. You want to be as close to the going rate as possible.

2. **Q:** *How do I structure my pricing in regards to seasons?*

    A: The Dominican Republic high season is generally December 12th-Apr 15 and July 1st-August 31st.

3. **Q:** *Should I allow pets?*

    A: While I wouldn't think that many people will be bringing their pet with them to the Dominican Republic, anything is possible. Allowing renters to bring pets could increase the amount of weeks the property is rented by giving you an advantage over your competition. If you do decide to allow pets I would make sure that you take an appropriate security deposit.

4. Q: *Should I charge by night or by person?*

A: In most cases if you are renting a condo you usually charge a flat per night fee. If you a renting a villa that can sleep many people many owners opt to charge an initial price for two people, and then add on charges for each additional guest. This can be a difficult thing to track especially when you are not living in the Dominican Republic or using a management company who can regulate this sort of thing. My recommendation is to always charge a per night fee. Potential renters seem to like this system better, and it allows you to get the full rate each time the property is booked.

5. Q: *Should I require a minimum stay?*

A: It is always to your advantage to require a minimum stay. This way you don't miss out on a potential week long rental because you rented the place out for one night in the middle of a week. Requiring a minimum stay of at least 3 nights will prevent you from constantly having to send a cleaning service in before the next rental.

6. Q: *Should I give discounts?*

A: For peak weeks I would not recommend giving out discounts. And normally I would not give discounts prior to one month before the rental. Why sell yourself short?

7. Q: *Should I charge my friends who want to rent my property?*

A: I would explain to your friends that if they want to reserve a week in advance that you have to charge them. And if it's a peek week you have to charge them full price. You should explain to them that by not charging them you are literally giving them $1500. You can tell them that if you have a last minute week unbooked that they are free to use it.

8. Q: *What is the best way to accept payments from renters?*

A: The most common way of accepting payments is personal checks. Paypal is becoming a more and more popular and secure way of accepting payments. Another preferred way of accepting payments is by credit card through a merchant account. These are the three methods I feel most comfortable with although other methods like cashier's checks, money orders, and wire transfers work too. Financially personal checks are the best method as there is no fee taken from your cut. But by accepting credit cards you may open yourself up to a larger audience of potential renters. The downside is that most merchant accounts will take a small percentage of the transaction as a fee.

9. **Q:** *Do I have to collect and pay sales tax for my rental?*

   A: Since the property is not in the US jurisdiction you do not have to pay any sales tax.

10. **Q:** *What is the best method for getting the key to the renter?*

    A: If you are using a management company they will take care of this for you. If you are not using a management company then the method I recommend is buying a combination key box. You can purchase one of these for under $50. You set up a combination on the box, place a key inside of it, and hang it on your door knob. You then give the renter the combination when you send them the information packet on the property.

11. **Q:** *How do I handle lost key situations?*

    A: A renter losing a key is something that will probably happen to you over the course of time. The best way to deal with this situation is to be prepared for it. My recommendation is to have a spare key hidden somewhere in the house or condo. You can keep this key in another lockbox inside a closet. Usually I would not give out this combination to the renter unless there is a need for it. Another option is to have a person located nearby who has a spare key. This person could be the same woman who cleans your property. You can arrange a fee ahead of time with her for when situations like this may arise. In the Dominican

158

Republic you can hire someone who will take care of this problem relatively cheap. And you can bill the renter the fee anyway.

12. Q: *What do I do about telephone and long-distance charges?*

 A: You can avoid long distance charges by putting a long distance blocker on your phone. This is available by local phone companies. In this case anyone using your property (including yourself) will be forced to use a calling card, cell phone, or service such as Skype for phone calls.

Chapter 13

Dominican Republic Country Information

Before investing, and possibly residing in the Dominican Republic, it is good to have some basic knowledge of the country itself. The following chapter is a collection of the most important information provided on the Dominican Republic by the State Department. While the information here may not be of use to you immediately, you can use this as a reference guide when questions come up.

People

Nationality: *Noun and adjective*--Dominican(s).
Population (2007): 9.365 million.
Annual growth rate (2007): 1.5%.
Ethnic groups: Mixed 73%, European 16%, African origin 11%.
Religion: Roman Catholic 95%.
Language: Spanish.
Education: *Years compulsory*--6 *Attendance*--70%. *Literacy*--84.7%.
Health: *Infant mortality rate:* 28.3/1,000. *Life expectancy*--70.2 years for men, 73.3 years for women.
Work force: 60.2% services (tourism, transportation, communications, finances, others), 15.5% industry (manufacturing), 11.5% construction, 11.3% agriculture, 1.5% mining.

Government

Type: Representative democracy.
Independence: February 27, 1844. Restoration of independence, August 16, 1863.

Constitution: November 28, 1966; amended July 25, 2002.
Branches: *Executive*--president (chief of state and head of government), vice president, cabinet. *Legislative*--bicameral Congress (Senate and House of Representatives). *Judicial*--Supreme Court of Justice.
Subdivisions: 31 provinces and the National District of Santo Domingo.
Political parties: Dominican Liberation Party (PLD), Dominican Revolutionary Party (PRD), Social Christian Reformist Party (PRSC), and several others.
Suffrage: Universal and compulsory, over 18 or married.

Economy (2006)

GDP: $36.05 billion.
Growth rate: 10.7%; (2007 est.: 7.9%).
Per capita GDP: $3,850.
Non-fuel minerals (1.4% of GDP): Nickel, gold, silver.
Agriculture (6.5% of GDP): *Products*--sugarcane, coffee, cocoa, bananas, tobacco, rice, plantains, beef.
Industry (27.4% of GDP): *Types*--sugar refining, pharmaceuticals, cement, light manufacturing, construction.
Services, including tourism and transportation: 58.6% of GDP.
Trade: *Exports* ($6.484 billion (FOB), including processing zones: textiles, sugar, coffee, ferronickel, cacao, tobacco, meats and medical supplies. *Markets*--U.S. (75%), Canada, Western Europe, South Korea. *Imports*--$8.797 billion: food stuffs, petroleum, industrial raw materials, capital goods. *Suppliers*--U.S. (48%), Japan, Germany, Venezuela, Mexico, Colombia.

PEOPLE
About half of Dominicans live in rural areas; many are small landholders. Haitians form the largest foreign minority group. All religions are tolerated; the state religion is Roman Catholicism.

Principal Government Officials

President--Leonel Fernández Reyna
Foreign Minister--Carlos Morales Troncoso
Ambassador to the United States--Flavio Dario Espinal Jacobo

Ambassador to the United Nations--Erasmo Lara Peña
Ambassador to the Organization of American States--Roberto Alvarez

The Dominican Republic maintains an embassy in the United States at 1715 22d Street NW, Washington, DC 20008 (tel. 202-332-6280).

ECONOMY

After a decade of little to no growth in the 1980s, the Dominican Republic's economy boomed in the 1990s, expanding at an average rate of 7.7% per year from 1996 to 2000. Tourism (the leading foreign exchange earner), telecommunications, and free-trade-zone manufacturing are the most important sectors, although agriculture is still a major part of the economy. The Dominican Republic owed much of its success to the adoption of sound macroeconomic policies in the early 1990s and greater opening to foreign investment. Growth turned negative in 2003 (-0.4%) due to the effects of government handling of major bank frauds and to lower U.S. demand for Dominican manufacturers. The Mejía administration negotiated an IMF standby agreement in August 2003 but was unable to comply with fiscal targets. The Fernández administration obtained required tax legislation and IMF board approval for the standby in January 2005. The Dominican peso fell to an unprecedented low in exchange markets in 2003-2004 but strengthened dramatically following the election and inauguration of Leonel Fernández. Since late 2004 it has traded at a rate considered to be overvalued on a purchasing power parity basis. Inflation fell sharply in late 2004 and was estimated at 9% for that calendar year. The Fernández administration successfully renegotiated official bilateral debt with Paris Club member governments, commercial bank debt with London Club members, and sovereign debt with a consortium of lenders. It met fiscal and financial targets of the standby agreement but fell short of goals for reforms in the electricity sector and financial markets. Central Bank statistics indicate 10.7% growth for 2006 with 5.0% inflation. The Central Bank estimates that the economy grew at 7.9% in the first six months of 2007 with an inflation rate of 5.9%.

The Dominican Republic's most important trading partner is the United States (75% of export revenues). Other markets include Canada, Western Europe, and Japan. The country exports free-trade-zone manufactured products (garments, medical devices, etc.), nickel, sugar, coffee, cacao, and tobacco. It imports petroleum, industrial raw materials, capital goods, and foodstuffs. On

September 5, 2005, the Dominican Congress ratified a free trade agreement with the U.S. and five Central American countries, known as CAFTA-DR. The CAFTA-DR agreement entered into force for the Dominican Republic on March 1, 2007. The total stock of U.S. foreign direct investment (FDI) in Dominican Republic as of 2006 was U.S. $3.3 billion, much of it directed to the energy and tourism sectors, to free trade zones, and to the telecommunications sector. Remittances were close to $2.7 billion in 2006.

An important aspect of the Dominican economy is the Free Trade Zone industry (FTZ), which made up U.S. $4.55 billion in Dominican exports for 2006 (70% of total exports). Reports show, however, that the FTZs lost approximately 60,000 between 2005 and 2007 and suffered a 4% decrease in total exports in 2006. The textiles sector experienced an approximate 17% drop in exports due in part to the appreciation of the Dominican peso against the dollar, Asian competition following expiration of the quotas of the Multi-Fiber Arrangement, and a government-mandated increase in salaries, which should have occurred in 2005 but was postponed to January 2006. Lost Dominican business was captured by firms in Central America and Asia. The tobacco, jewelry, medical, and pharmaceutical sectors in the FTZs all reported increases for 2006, which somewhat offset textile and garment losses. Industry experts from the FTZs expect that entry into force of the CAFTA-DR agreement will promote substantial growth in the FTZ sector for 2007.

An ongoing concern in the Dominican Republic is the inability of participants in the electricity sector to establish financial viability for the system. Three regional electricity distribution systems were privatized in 1998 via sale of 50% of shares to foreign operators; the Mejía administration repurchased all foreign-owned shares in two of these systems in late 2003. The third, serving the eastern provinces, is operated by U.S. concerns and is 50% U.S.-owned. The World Bank records that electricity distribution losses for 2005 totaled about 38.2%, a rate of losses exceeded in only three other countries. Industry experts estimate distribution losses for 2006 will surpass 40%, primarily due to low collection rates, theft, infrastructure problems and corruption. At the close of 2006, the government had exceeded its budget for electricity subsidies, spending close to U.S. $650 million. The government plans to continue providing subsidies. Congress passed a law in 2007 that criminalizes the act of stealing electricity, but it has not yet been fully implemented. The electricity sector is a highly politicized sector and with 2008 presidential election campaigning already in motion, the prospect of further effective reforms of the electricity sector is poor. Debts in the sector, including government debt, amount to more than U.S. $500 million. Some generating companies are undercapitalized and at times unable to purchase adequate fuel supplies

U.S.-DOMINICAN REPUBLIC RELATIONS

The U.S. has a strong interest in a democratic, stable, and economically healthy Dominican Republic. The country's standing as the largest Caribbean economy, second-largest country in terms of population and land mass, with large bilateral trade with the United States, and its proximity to the United States and other smaller Caribbean nations make the Dominican Republic an important partner in hemispheric affairs. The Embassy estimates that 100,000 U.S. citizens live in the Dominican Republic; many are dual nationals. An important element of the relationship between the two countries is the fact that more than 1 million individuals of Dominican origin reside in the United States, most of them in the metropolitan Northeast and some in Florida.

U.S. relations with the Dominican Republic are excellent, and the U.S. has been an outspoken supporter of that country's democratic and economic development. The Dominican Government has been supportive of many U.S. initiatives in the United Nations and related agencies. The two governments cooperate in the fight against the traffic in illegal substances. The Dominican Republic has worked closely with U.S. law enforcement officials on issues such as the extradition of fugitives and measures to hinder illegal migration.

The United States supports the Fernández administration's efforts to improve Dominican competitiveness, to attract foreign private investment, to fight corruption, and to modernize the tax system. Bilateral trade is important to both countries. U.S. firms, mostly manufacturers of apparel, footwear, and light electronics, as well as U.S. energy companies, account for much of the foreign private investment in the Dominican Republic.

Exports from the United States, including those from Puerto Rico and the U.S. Virgin Islands, to the Dominican Republic in 2005 totaled $5.3 billion, up 11% from the previous year. The Dominican Republic exported $4.5 billion to the United States in 2006, equaling some 75% of its export revenues. The Dominican Republic is the 47th-largest commercial partner of the U.S. The U.S. Embassy works closely with U.S. business firms and Dominican trade groups, both of which can take advantage of the new opportunities in this growing market. At the same time, the Embassy is working with the Dominican Government to resolve a range of ongoing commercial and investment disputes.

The Embassy counsels U.S. firms through its Country Commercial Guide and informally via meetings with business persons planning to invest or already investing in the Dominican Republic. This is a challenging business environment for U.S. firms, especially for medium to smaller sized businesses.

The U.S. Agency for International Development (USAID) mission is focused on improving access of underserved populations to quality health care and combating HIV/AIDS and tuberculosis (TB); , promoting economic growth through policy reform, support for CAFTA-DR implementation, and technical assistance to small producers and tourism groups; environmental protection and policy reform initiatives; improved access to quality primary, public education and assistance to at-risk youth; a model rural electrification program; and improving participation in democratic processes, while strengthening the judiciary and combating corruption across all sectors.

Important Contact Information

U.S. Department of Commerce
International Trade Administration
Trade Information Center
14th and Constitution Avenue, NW
Washington, DC 20230
Tel: 1-800-USA-TRADE
Internet: http://trade.gov/

Caribbean/Latin American Action
1818 N. Street, NW, Suite 310
Washington, DC 20036
Tel: (202) 466-7464
Fax: (202) 822-0075

American Chamber of Commerce in the Dominican Republic
Torre Empresarial, 6to.
Piso, Ave. Sarasota No. 25,
Santo Domingo, Dominican Republic
Tel: (809) 381-0777
Fax: (809) 381-0303

E-mail: amcham@codetel.net.do
Home Page: http://www.amcham.org.do

Appendix

Dominican Real Estate Companies

Carribean Real Estate Investment Group
www.mydrlife.com

Remax Coral Bay Real Estate
Plaza del Sol
Calle del Ayuntamiento, Sosua,
Dominican RepublicTel: 1-809-571-3348
Tel: 1-809-571-9990
Fax: 1-809-571-9991
http://www.coralbayrealestate.com

Bruce Pierson.
DR Paradise / Homes, Villas and Estates
Homepages: www.drparadise.com & www.drcaribbean.net/
Email: bruce@drparadise.com
Telephone/Fax 1-809-240-6054 (D.R.)
Cellular:1-809-910-4190
USA: Voice over IP- 1-(908)-212-7524.

Coldwell Banker North Coast
Calle Alejo Martinez No. 1
Plaza Colonial (next to Banco Popular)
Sosua, El Batey
Phone: 001-809-571-2324
Fax: 001-809-571-2511
Email: info@coldwellbanker-northcoast.com
www.coldwellbanker-northcoast.com

Jaun Perdoma Punta Cana

www.juanperdomo.com/punta-cana/

Trust Realty

Plaza Trust, Av. Alemania 91
(Between Plaza El Dorado & EdenH Resort)
Bàvaro-Punta Cana
Phone: (1) 809-552-1777
       (1) 877-718-3817 (Toll Free)
Fax: (1) 866-437-7269
Email: trustrealty@punta-cana.us
 Web: www.punta-cana.us

Dominican Republic Real Estate Financing

Aceltis Financial Group
Phone: 973-638-2466
Fax: 440-508-1225
Toll-free: 877-775-1626

www.aceltisgroup.com

Dominican Republic Rental Sites

VRBO.com- this site charges a yearly fee of $179 to run your ad for the year. There are upgrades that you can opt for that will let you add more photos. This is one of my favorite sites to use when searching for a property to rent. The site has been around for awhile and it gets heavy traffic.

Escape Artist.com- This very popular site is among the least expensive at only $99 a year. The site also allows you up to 20 images. The only draw back of this site is that it is not exclusively a rental site, and can be a little difficult to navigate from the home page.

VacationRentals.com- Another site that gets heavy traffic, and gives you a one year ad for $148. There ad comes with eight photos and an availability calendar.

A1Vacations.com- This site has two options: 12 months with 4 photos for $148 or 12 months with 12 photos for $178.

Home Away.com- This $299 package gets you listed on 5 sites for 12 months with 12 photos. The sites that you get listed on are Home Away, Cyber Rentals, Great Rentals, and A1 Vacations

VacationRentals411.com- This site is free for you basic listing which includes 9 photos. There are upgrade packages available that let you add many more features.

www.ingramcontent.com/pod-product-compliance
Lightning Source LLC
Chambersburg PA
CBHW031810190326
41518CB00006B/279